Understanding Your Limits

Knowing Boundaries for a Responsible and Fulfilling Life

By Sami Dayriyeh

Disclaimer

Copyright © the Year 2024

All Rights Reserved.

No part of this book can be transmitted or reproduced in any form, including print, electronic, photocopying, scanning, mechanical, or recording, without prior written permission from the author.

While the author has made utmost efforts to ensure the accuracy of the written content, all readers are advised to follow the information mentioned herein at their own risk. The author cannot be held responsible for any personal or commercial damage caused by the misinterpretation of information. All readers are encouraged to seek professional advice when needed.

This book has been written for information purposes only. Every effort has been made to make this book as complete and accurate as possible. However, there may be mistakes in typography or content. Also, this book provides information only up to the publishing date. Therefore, this book should be used as a guide - not as the ultimate source.

The stories in this book are based on real-life events, but fictional names have been used for privacy and confidentiality reasons.

The purpose of this book is to educate. The author and the publisher do not warrant that the information contained in this book is fully complete and shall not be responsible for any errors or omissions. The author and publisher shall have neither liability nor responsibility to any person or entity with respect to any loss or damage caused or alleged to be caused directly or indirectly by this book.

Table of Contents

Preface 1
Chapter 1: Embracing Your Personal Limits 3
   Tasha's Reflection: Taking a Step Back to Thrive 4
   The Positive Effects of Accepting Personal Limits 6
      Psychological Well-Being 6
      Resilience and Coping 7
      Reduced Stress and Anxiety 8
   Practical Exercises for Accepting Personal Boundaries 10
      Journaling 10
      Clarify Your Values 11
      Learn to Say No 12
      Self-Compassion Exercises 13
Chapter 2: Pushing Past the Boundaries 15
   Brushstrokes of Growth: Arthur Pushes Past the Boundaries
.... 15
   Conquering Dyslexia, Shyness, and Introversion Challenges 16
      Dyslexia 17
      Shyness and Social Anxiety 18
      Introversion 19
   Holistic Strategies for Expanding Your Boundaries 20
      Self-Acceptance 20
      Take Courageous Initiatives 21
      Practice Continuously 23
      Brainstorming and Debating 24
      Advocate for Yourself 25

- Develop Social Skills 26
- Establish Boundaries 28
- Choose Social Activities Wisely 29
- Leverage Your Strengths 30

Chapter 3: Empowerment Within Bounds: Acknowledging Your Limits 32

- Chelsea's Aspirations: A Journey of Success 32
- Significance of Acknowledged Limits and Empowerment 34
  - Decision-Making and Goal-Setting 34
  - Strength-Based Approach 36
  - Gender Empowerment 37
- Tips to Achieve Self-Empowerment 38
  - Cultivate a Positive Attitude 38
  - Set Reasonable Goals 39
  - Skill Enhancement 40
  - Build a Support System 42
  - Campaigning and Lobbying 42

Chapter 4: Professional Ethics and Client Relations 45

- Ethical Dilemma: Dr. Mitchell's Unveiling 45
- Significance of Maintaining Ethical Boundaries with Clients . 47
  - Enhancing Trust and Safety 47
  - Ethical and Legal Standards 48
  - Promoting Objectivity 50
- How to Maintain Professional Boundaries with Clients 51
  - Establish Clear Policies and Informed Consent 51
  - Establish Clear Communication Channels 53

    Maintain Professional Demeanor 54

    Respect Personal Space 55

    Be Mindful of Dual Relationships 56

    Set Boundaries for Gifts and Favors 57

Chapter 5: Navigating Technology and Digital Boundaries 59

    Unplugged in the City: Rebecca Navigates Digital Boundaries 59

    Impact of Technology on Mental Health and Privacy 61

        Mental Health 61

        Privacy 62

        Positive Impact 63

    Tips for Navigating Digital Boundaries 64

        Set Clear Limits 65

        Manage Notifications 66

        Audit Your Digital Presence 67

        Digital Detox Days 68

        Prioritize Real-Life Connections 68

Chapter 6: Competence and Qualifications 70

    A Well-Intentioned Misstep: Dr. Morgan Crosses the Line ... 70

    The Consequences of Professional Malpractice and Negligence 72

        Sanctions 72

        Impact on Patient Safety and Trust 73

        Reputational Damage 74

    Learning to Stay Within Your Area of Expertise 76

        Recognize Your Limits 76

Stay Up to Date 77
Collaborate with Experts 78
Clearly Define the Scope of Work 79
Evaluate Risks and Consequences 79

Chapter 7: Authority and Jurisdiction 81
Breach of Trust: Vivian's Downfall 81
Consequences of Stepping Outside Authority and Jurisdiction
.... 82
Economic Decline 83
Erosion of Trust and Legitimacy 84
Reputational Damage 85
Understanding and Respecting Authority and Jurisdiction ... 86
Stay Informed About Laws and Regulations 86
Know the Chain of Command 87
Seek Permissions and Authorizations 88
Promote a Speak-Up Culture 88
Lead By Example 89
Understand Professional Ethics 90
Seek Feedback 91

Chapter 8: Overstepped Boundaries 94
Boundaries Unseen: Jamie Learns a Lesson in Respect 94
Signs of Overstepped Boundaries 95
Codependency 96
Deteriorating Relationships 97
Guilt 98
How to Respect Boundaries and Limits Set By Others 99

    Always Ask for Consent 100

    Observe Nonverbal Cues 101

    Respect Emotional Boundaries 102

    Accept 'No' Gracefully 103

    Be Mindful of Social Media 104

    Apologize and Learn 105

    Create Mutual Agreements 106

Chapter 9: Negotiating Ethical Crossroads in Life 108

  Bound By Integrity: Ted's Decision 108

  Significance of Ethical Boundaries 109

    Trust and Reputation 110

    Individual Well-Being 111

    Social Responsibility 112

  Navigating Ethical Dilemmas with Integrity 113

    Define Your Values 114

    Consider Consequences 115

    Seek Different Perspectives 116

    Consider the Golden Rule 117

    Take Your Time 118

    Be Prepared to Take Responsibility 118

    Consider the "Front-Page Test" 119

Chapter 10: Balancing Work and Life 121

  Balancing Act: Sarah's Journey 121

  Importance of Maintaining a Healthy Work-Life Balance ... 123

    Reduced Stress and Burnout 123

    Positive Impact on Mental Health 124

- Enhanced Family and Social Relationships 125
- How to Create Work-Life Balance 127
  - Establish Work and Personal Boundaries 127
  - Create a Realistic Schedule 128
  - Create a Dedicated Workspace 129
  - Delegate and Outsource 130
  - Take Vacation Time 131
  - Communicate Openly 132
- Chapter 11: Thriving Within Limits: The Role of Self-Reflection 133
  - Adapt and Inspire: Marcus's Journey 133
  - How Self-Reflection Leads to Personal Growth 134
    - Clarification of Values and Goals 135
    - Improved Problem-Solving Skills 136
    - Mindfulness-Based Interventions 137
  - Exercises for Self-Reflection and Personal Development 138
    - Journaling 139
    - Mindfulness Meditation 140
    - The Five Whys 140
    - Strengths Assessment 141
    - Gratitude Practice 142
    - Life Wheel Assessment 143
    - Silence and Solitude 144
- Chapter 12: Nurturing Respectful Boundaries in Life 146
  - The Recovery of Respect: A Company's Transformation 146

Importance of Boundary Setting and Empathy in
Organizations 148
   Increased Productivity 148
   Positive Work Environment 150
How to Foster Respectful Boundaries at Workplaces 151
   Clearly Define Expectations 152
   Promote Work-Life Balance 153
   Flexible Working Arrangements 154
   Training on Boundaries 155
   Encourage Breaks 156
   Promote Self-Care 157

Postface 159
References 161
About the Author 166

Preface

Limits, in a broad sense, refer to the boundaries, constraints, or restrictions that define the extent of something. These boundaries can be physical, emotional, intellectual, or ethical, and they play a crucial role in various aspects of life.

However, there exists a fundamental truth: knowing your limits is not a proclamation of inadequacy but a celebration of your uniqueness. In a world that often glorifies comparison, become true to yourself and embrace the beauty of individuality.

Understanding Your Limits is a guidebook that seeks to illuminate the significance of recognizing, embracing, and navigating the boundaries that define your individual and collective spaces. It encourages you not only to acknowledge your limits but to understand them as the launching pad to strive for your own betterment.

Whether you're after personal or professional growth, it's important to acknowledge that every journey is shaped by limits. This acknowledgment, far from stifling ambition, is the basis upon which true success, contentment, and confidence are built. This book explores the nuanced art of discerning these limits and harnessing their wisdom to lead a life of fulfillment without ever crossing the line.

Consider this a gentle reminder: don't chastise yourself for not achieving as much as someone else. You are unique with your own strengths, quirks, and capabilities. Each individual, with their capabilities and traits, holds within them a reservoir of untapped potential. The key lies in understanding these nuances, recognizing their limitations, and then boldly pushing against those limits to expand capabilities continuously.

The pages that follow are not a call to complacency but rather a beacon guiding you through the delicate balance between pushing your boundaries and respecting the boundaries of others. It is a roadmap for professionals, yet its wisdom is universal, catering to individuals from all walks of life who strive to live authentically, harmoniously, and within ethical bounds.

Each chapter unfolds stories that resonate with human experience, research findings that shed light on the psychological, sociological, and ethical dimensions of setting and respecting limits, and practical strategies that empower readers to navigate the intricate web of relationships, be it with peers, colleagues, clients, or within contractual agreements.

This book is not merely a collection of principles; it is a holistic guide that encourages readers to reflect on their own lives, relationships, and professions. It is a call to action, urging individuals to embrace their specialized roles, competencies, and authorities responsibly. In doing so, you not only protect yourself from legal pitfalls and professional missteps but also contribute to the creation of a more just, respectful, and harmonious society.

Chapter 1: Embracing Your Personal Limits

Personal limits refer to invisible boundaries you set for yourself, delineating the contours of your values, beliefs, and comfort zones. These limits extend their influence across diverse spheres of your life, from the intricacies of relationships and the demands of the workplace to the delicate balance of personal well-being and ethical considerations.

But, establishing personal limits is an act of self-acknowledgment and respect. It is a declaration that your values matter, your beliefs are significant, and your well-being is non-negotiable. By consciously defining these limits, individuals commit to a life guided by principles that resonate with their true selves.

Respecting personal limits is not merely a matter of convenience; it is an embodiment of integrity. It reflects an unwavering commitment to staying true to oneself even when faced with external pressures or societal expectations. This commitment, in turn, fortifies a profound sense of self-respect—an understanding that honoring personal boundaries is an act of self-love.

Life is full of setbacks and challenges; sometimes, they may as well be inevitable. However, the art lies in recognizing that not every obstacle is a personal failure. You can't blame yourself or others for something that is beyond your personal limits.

Comparison is not only futile but detrimental to one's well-being. Thriving doesn't come from conforming to external standards but from understanding and appreciating the distinctive qualities that make each person who they are.

Let's understand the significance of embracing your limits with the help of a story.

Tasha's Reflection: Taking a Step Back to Thrive

Tasha was a resilient go-getter, always pushing herself to excel in her career, maintain thriving relationships, and uphold an image of perfection working at a demanding corporate firm.

Surrounded by ambitious colleagues and tight deadlines, Tasha constantly compared her progress to others, attributing every missed opportunity to her perceived shortcomings. The weight of unmet expectations bore heavily on her shoulders, casting a shadow over her accomplishments.

One time, while working on a complex project with tight deadlines and high stakes, Tasha finally had a moment of self-reflection.

Tasha, driven by her relentless pursuit of success, poured her heart and soul into this particular project. Long nights at the office became routine as she navigated intricate details, collaborated with colleagues, and strategized to ensure the project's success.

As the deadline approached, unforeseen challenges arose—market fluctuations, unexpected technical issues, and last-minute changes in client expectations. Despite Tasha's tireless efforts, the project encountered setbacks that were beyond her control. The culmination of these challenges led to an outcome that fell short of the initially envisioned success.

In the aftermath of the project, the atmosphere at the office was tense. Tasha found herself caught in a whirlwind of emotions, grappling with disappointment, frustration, and an overwhelming sense of failure. The weight of unmet expectations bore heavily on her shoulders, and the whispers of self-blame echoed in her thoughts.

It was in this moment of professional turbulence that Tasha felt a need to pause and reassess. Rather than succumbing to the familiar spiral of self-blame, she chose to step back and reflect.

She realized that, despite her best efforts, some factors were beyond her control—market fluctuations, unforeseen challenges, and the unpredictable nature of human interactions. It was a moment of clarity that sparked a transformative shift in her mindset.

Determined to break free from the shackles of self-blame, Tasha began a journey of self-discovery. She started accepting and embracing her personal limits. More importantly, she unearthed the concept of embracing personal limits as a source of strength rather than weakness.

Instead of berating herself for every perceived failure, Tasha started recognizing the boundaries of her capabilities. She acknowledged that she couldn't control every outcome, and that was okay. It was a revelation that allowed her to redirect her energy toward aspects of her life that were within her control—nurturing genuine connections, investing in her well-being, and pursuing goals aligned with her values.

As Tasha embraced her personal limits, she noticed a profound shift. The weight on her shoulders lifted, replaced by a newfound sense of freedom. She thrived within the bounds of her authenticity, finding joy in the journey rather than fixating on the destination. Her career blossomed, her relationships deepened, and, most importantly, her self-worth soared.

The Positive Effects of Accepting Personal Limits

In a world where everyone strives for personal growth and well-being, one aspect that is often overlooked is the act of accepting personal limits.

Embracing personal limits leads to resilience, balance, and self-discovery. The journey toward understanding and embracing our own boundaries is a transformative one, marked by the recognition that true strength lies not only in expanding your limits but also in acknowledging the limits themselves.

That said, let's look at insightful research findings that highlight the positive effects of accepting personal limits.

Psychological Well-Being

The link between setting and accepting personal limits and psychological well-being has been a focal point in numerous studies, shedding light on the profound impact that establishing clear boundaries can have on an individual's mental health. These investigations consistently reveal a positive correlation between the practice of setting personal limits and various markers of psychological well-being.

One pivotal study conducted by Baumeister et al. in 2007 delves into the intricate mechanisms that underlie the relationship between personal boundaries and mental well-being. According to their findings, self-regulation emerges as a key player in this dynamic. Self-regulation refers to the ability to manage one's thoughts, emotions, and behaviors effectively, and the study suggests that setting personal limits is a crucial aspect of this self-regulatory process.

The research underscores the idea that establishing and respecting personal limits acts as a form of self-regulation, allowing individuals to navigate the complexities of life more effectively. By defining what is acceptable and what exceeds one's capacity, individuals can conserve mental resources, preventing the depletion of cognitive and emotional energy.

Furthermore, the preservation of mental resources through boundary-setting contributes to a reduction in stress levels. When individuals establish clear limits on their time, energy, and emotional investments, they create a buffer against the overwhelming demands of daily life. This, in turn, fosters a sense of control and autonomy, key components of psychological well-being.

Increased resilience is another noteworthy outcome associated with the establishment of personal limits. The ability to bounce back from challenges and setbacks is closely tied to an individual's capacity to set and uphold boundaries. By doing so, individuals create a protective barrier that shields them from excessive stressors, enabling them to better withstand life's inevitable adversities.

Resilience and Coping
Research by Bonanno (2004) delves into the intricate relationship between accepting personal limitations and the demonstration of higher levels of resilience, especially in the face of adversity.

Resilience, in the psychological context, refers to an individual's capacity to bounce back from challenging or traumatic experiences. Bonanno's work suggests that the acceptance of personal limitations plays a pivotal role in enhancing this resilience. Rather than viewing limitations as weaknesses, individuals who acknowledge and accept their inherent constraints develop a more adaptive and nuanced approach to coping with life's adversities.

Acceptance of personal limitations involves recognizing the aspects of life that are beyond one's control. Bonanno proposes that this recognition becomes a foundation for the development of adaptive coping mechanisms. When individuals acknowledge that certain challenges are inevitable and beyond their sphere of influence, they are more likely to employ coping strategies that focus on navigating and adapting to the situation rather than resisting or denying it.

Individuals who embrace their personal limits exhibit a psychological flexibility that allows them to navigate adversity more effectively. Rather than being paralyzed by the uncontrollable aspects of a situation, they are more likely to adjust their mindset and actions in response to the challenges at hand. This adaptability is a key component of resilience.

One of the significant outcomes of accepting personal limitations is a reduced stress response to uncontrollable situations. Bonanno's research implies that individuals who accept their limits are less likely to experience prolonged distress or anxiety when faced with adversity. This reduced stress response contributes to better mental health outcomes and facilitates a quicker recovery from challenging circumstances.

Moreover, acceptance of personal limits fosters a more holistic approach to well-being. Instead of fixating on what cannot be changed, individuals are more likely to invest energy in aspects of their lives that are within their control. This shift in focus contributes to a more balanced and adaptive approach to life, enhancing overall psychological resilience.

Reduced Stress and Anxiety

The study conducted by Hayes, Luoma, Bond, Masuda, and Lillis in 2006 sheds light on the profound impact of accepting limitations and uncertainties on reducing stress and anxiety.

This therapeutic approach, known as Acceptance and Commitment Therapy (ACT), emphasizes embracing what cannot be changed and fostering a more balanced emotional response to life's challenges.

The study underscores the fundamental principle of ACT, which is the acceptance of thoughts, feelings, and circumstances without unnecessary attempts to control or change them. Specifically, the research emphasizes that accepting limitations is an integral aspect of this acceptance-based model.

One of the central tenets of ACT is the concept of psychological flexibility, defined as the ability to be open, adaptable, and effective in the presence of changing and unpredictable events. Accepting limitations contributes to reduced psychological rigidity, allowing individuals to respond to life's uncertainties with greater adaptability.

Moreover, ACT incorporates mindfulness and present-moment awareness as essential components. Acceptance of limitations encourages individuals to be fully present in the current moment rather than ruminating on the past or anxiously anticipating the future. This shift in focus contributes to a more balanced emotional state.

The study also suggests that accepting limitations within the ACT framework reduces avoidance behaviors. Instead of evading or suppressing challenging thoughts or emotions, individuals learn to accept them without judgment. This shift leads to a more balanced emotional response, mitigating the impact of stress and anxiety.

Accepting limitations within the ACT model is not a passive resignation but an active acknowledgment. The study indicates that this acknowledgment paves the way for individuals to redirect their energy toward actions that align with their core values. As a result, they engage in purposeful and meaningful activities, contributing to overall well-being.

The research concludes that as individuals adopt an acceptance-based approach, they experience a reduction in stress and anxiety. By letting go of the futile struggle against uncontrollable aspects of life, individuals can cultivate a more balanced emotional response, fostering a sense of calmness even in the face of uncertainty.

Practical Exercises for Accepting Personal Boundaries

Boundaries, both internal and external, define the space where your authenticity thrives. As such, the concept of personal boundaries has emerged as a guiding force, shaping the contours of the emotional landscape. To truly understand and honor yourself, it is essential to engage in the art of accepting and asserting personal boundaries.

That said, here are some practical strategies that can help you accept personal limits without falling into the spiral of blame:

Journaling

Journaling serves as a powerful tool that leads to the acceptance of personal limits. It provides a structured and introspective space to navigate the complexities of your emotional terrain. Through this intentional practice, individuals can cultivate self-awareness, explore the contours of their boundaries, and ultimately foster a sense of acceptance for the unique limits that shape their authentic selves.

Begin by establishing a dedicated time each day for journaling. Consistency is key in creating a ritual that becomes an integral part of your routine, offering a sanctuary for self-reflection.

Delve into situations where discomfort or stress surfaced during your day. Be specific and honest in recounting these moments. Reflect on the emotions they elicited and the circumstances surrounding them.

Use your journal to identify instances where personal boundaries may have been crossed. This could include feeling overwhelmed, pressured, or disrespected. Write down the details of these situations to gain clarity on the nature of the boundary violations.

Over time, observe patterns in your journal entries. Are there recurring themes or specific triggers that consistently challenge your boundaries? Recognizing these patterns provides valuable insights into the areas of your life where acceptance of personal limits may be particularly beneficial.

Remember, journaling is an opportunity to practice self-compassion. As you reflect on challenging moments, offer yourself kindness and understanding. Acknowledge that personal limits are a natural part of being human and that it's okay to set and enforce boundaries.

Clarify Your Values
Create a comprehensive list of your core values—those guiding principles that reflect your beliefs, priorities, and what matters most to you. These values can encompass areas such as integrity, compassion, creativity, family, autonomy, or personal growth.

Take intentional time to reflect on various situations in your life where you have felt a sense of discomfort or unease. These could be instances where decisions or actions seemed to clash with your inherent values.

Consider the external pressures or societal expectations that may have influenced your choices in these situations. Was there a conflict between what you believed to be right and the expectations imposed by others or societal norms?

Identify specific instances where you compromised your core values under external pressure. This could involve conforming to societal norms, adhering to expectations at work, or succumbing to the opinions of others. Be honest and detailed in your reflections.

Explore your emotional responses in these situations. Did you experience discomfort, guilt, or a sense of inner conflict? Understanding the emotional impact of compromising your values provides valuable insights into the significance of these principles in your life.

Through reflection, clarify where your personal boundaries lie concerning each core value. Consider what actions or situations are non-negotiable when it comes to honoring these values. This clarity becomes the foundation for setting and asserting boundaries in the future.

Moving forward, set intentions for upholding your core values. Use your reflections as a guide to assert boundaries that safeguard these principles. Communicate your values clearly to others, and make choices that align with your authentic self, even in the face of external pressures.

Learn to Say No

Practice saying "no" assertively and without guilt in low-stakes situations. This could involve simple requests or invitations that don't carry significant weight. Recognizing these scenarios provides a safe space for practicing assertiveness.

At the same time, acknowledge that saying "no" is a powerful tool for setting boundaries and maintaining a sense of control over your time, energy, and commitments. Embrace the idea that declining certain requests is a valid and necessary act of self-care.

Internalize the notion that it's acceptable to say "no" when something is beyond your control or falls outside your comfort zone. Recognize that acknowledging limitations is not a sign of weakness but a demonstration of self-awareness and self-respect. Cultivate the awareness to discern situations where your refusal is a proactive measure to avoid crossing your personal boundaries. Understand that chasing after opportunities or commitments that may compromise your well-being is counterproductive in the long run.

After each assertive "no," take a moment to reflect on your emotional responses. Note any feelings of guilt or discomfort that may arise. This self-awareness allows you to address and overcome potential emotional barriers associated with setting boundaries.

Self-Compassion Exercises
Everyone faces challenges, limitations, and moments of struggle. The important thing is to embrace the fact that experiencing difficulties is a shared aspect of the human experience. This recognition forms the foundation of self-compassion.

Practice shifting your perspective from self-criticism to self-compassion. Instead of berating yourself for perceived shortcomings or limitations, acknowledge that these are natural aspects of being human. Embrace a kinder, more understanding stance toward yourself.

Engage in mindful self-compassion exercises. These exercises often involve guided meditations or affirmations that encourage a gentle and nurturing attitude toward oneself, fostering a non-judgmental approach.

Pay special attention to your internal dialogue. When facing challenges or recognizing your limitations, consciously choose words and phrases that reflect kindness and understanding. Consider how you would speak to a friend in a similar situation and extend that same level of compassion to yourself.

Develop self-compassionate affirmations that counteract negative self-talk. Affirmations such as "I am doing my best," "It's okay to have limits," or "I deserve kindness and understanding" serve as reminders of your inherent worth and the importance of self-compassion.

You can always write self-compassionate letters to yourself. Address these letters as if you were writing to a dear friend facing challenges. Express understanding, kindness, and encouragement. This practice fosters a written record of self-compassion that can be revisited during difficult times.

But more than anything else, embrace the concept of imperfection as a natural part of the human experience. Understand that having limitations or facing challenges does not diminish your value. Practice self-compassion by acknowledging that it's okay not to be perfect and that growth often comes from navigating difficulties.

Remember that the exercises mentioned above are somewhat of a journey, and progress takes time. Consistent practice will contribute to a deeper understanding of personal boundaries and the development of a more authentic and fulfilling life.

Chapter 2: Pushing Past the Boundaries

Recognizing one's limits is crucial, yet they should not be perceived as constraints. Rather than serving as confinements, limits can be viewed as dynamic markers ready to be pushed further.

Evolving into an enhanced version of yourself necessitates the intentional expansion of these boundaries. Embracing the opportunity to stretch beyond your current limits is a pivotal step toward personal growth and self-improvement.

But, individual limits vary from person to person. The process of expanding personal boundaries is a highly individualized endeavor, and there's value in recognizing and respecting the diverse paces at which people choose to navigate this transformative path.

Remember, personal growth is not a one-size-fits-all concept; it thrives when you embrace the fluidity of your own limits and embark on the journey to expand them at a pace aligned with your personal rhythm.

That said, let's understand the concept of pushing past boundaries with the help of a story.

Brushstrokes of Growth: Arthur Pushes Past the Boundaries

Arthur was a shy and introverted teenager living in Maplewood, New Jersey. Making friends and talking to people were the most difficult things Arthur had to do. Rather than pushing himself to try, Arthur sought comfort in his own company. Ultimately, that led him to the town's library, where books became a safe haven.

While turning the pages, Arthur wanted to connect with others. But talking to people seemed hard. The social rules felt like a tricky area where words got mixed up, and conversations didn't go smoothly.

One day, Arthur discovered an art class at the community center. This class turned out to be a special place where he could be around people without worrying about striking up a conversation. With every stroke of the paintbrush, Arthur felt more at ease. It was like a secret language that helped express feelings without stumbling over words.

As the art class became routine, Arthur started feeling more confident. Slowly, talking to others didn't seem as scary. The people in the town were friendly and supportive, making it easier for him to take small steps outside his comfort zone.

With newfound confidence, Arthur began helping out at local events. The once-quiet person started enjoying conversations and even found a way to tell stories despite his shyness.

Through the struggles of shyness and introversion, Arthur discovered that personal growth happens one step at a time, creating a beautiful picture of self-discovery.

Conquering Dyslexia, Shyness, and Introversion Challenges

Navigating the challenges posed by dyslexia, shyness, and introversion requires a nuanced understanding of individual experiences and targeted interventions.

Over the years, researchers have delved into various strategies to overcome these obstacles, seeking effective approaches that foster personal growth and well-being.

That said, let's see how people with dyslexia, shyness, and introversion can expand their boundaries by looking at some insightful research findings.

Dyslexia

The research conducted by the National Reading Panel in 2000 stands as a landmark in understanding effective interventions for individuals with dyslexia. Their findings notably highlighted the efficacy of phonics-based interventions in enhancing reading skills among this population.

Phonics-based approaches involve teaching individuals to associate sounds with letters or groups of letters, emphasizing the relationship between letters and their corresponding sounds.

Furthermore, the Orton-Gillingham approach, a multisensory method, has gained widespread recognition for its effectiveness in teaching individuals with dyslexia. Named after its creators, Samuel Orton and Anna Gillingham, this approach places a strong emphasis on engaging multiple senses in the learning process. It recognizes that individuals with dyslexia may benefit from approaches that go beyond traditional visual or auditory methods.

In the Orton-Gillingham approach, lessons are structured to incorporate tactile and kinesthetic elements, such as writing letters in sand or using physical objects to represent sounds. By engaging multiple senses simultaneously, this approach aims to strengthen the connections between language and sensory experiences, making the learning process more accessible and effective for individuals with dyslexia.

The underlying principle is to provide a comprehensive and individualized learning experience that accommodates the diverse needs of learners with dyslexia. By combining auditory, visual, and tactile-kinesthetic elements, these interventions create a supportive environment for individuals with dyslexia to grasp and retain essential reading skills. The emphasis on a multisensory approach aligns with the understanding that people with dyslexia may benefit from varied methods of instruction tailored to their unique learning styles and strengths.

Shyness and Social Anxiety

The research conducted by Heimberg et al., 1998 has significantly contributed to our understanding of effective interventions for social anxiety and shyness. Their work focused on cognitive behavioral therapy (CBT) as a therapeutic approach and showcased its efficacy in addressing the challenges associated with these conditions.

Cognitive-behavioral therapy is a structured and goal-oriented therapeutic approach that explores the connections between thoughts, feelings, and behaviors.

In the context of social anxiety and shyness, individuals often grapple with negative thought patterns and perceptions about themselves in social situations. CBT aims to identify and modify these negative cognitions, fostering more adaptive and constructive ways of thinking.

CBT involves helping individuals recognize and understand their negative thought patterns related to social interactions. These thoughts may include fears of judgment, rejection, or embarrassment.

Once identified, individuals work with therapists to challenge and reframe these negative thoughts. This process, known as cognitive restructuring, aims to replace irrational or distorted thoughts with more realistic and positive ones.

CBT often incorporates exposure techniques, where individuals gradually face and confront feared social situations. This exposure is done in a systematic and controlled manner, allowing individuals to build confidence and reduce anxiety over time.

Adaptive behaviors and social skills are also emphasized in CBT. Individuals learn and practice effective communication, assertiveness, and problem-solving skills, providing them with tools to navigate social situations more comfortably.

Between sessions, individuals typically engage in homework assignments that reinforce the skills learned during therapy. This helps integrate therapeutic strategies into real-life situations.

Introversion

Susan Cain's work, particularly highlighted in her 2012 book "Quiet: The Power of Introverts in a World That Can't Stop Talking," has been instrumental in reshaping the narrative around introversion.

Cain advocates for recognizing and embracing introversion as a natural and valuable aspect of personality rather than viewing it negatively. This perspective challenges societal norms that often prioritize extroverted qualities.

By acknowledging introversion as a valid and valuable trait, individuals can experience a positive impact on their well-being. This shift in perception encourages introverts to appreciate their strengths, such as deep thinking, focused work, and meaningful reflection.

Cain suggests that introverts can benefit from developing adaptation strategies to navigate a predominantly extroverted world. These strategies may include finding quiet spaces for focused work, creating environments conducive to introspection, and scheduling downtime to recharge after social interactions.

Introverts may find it beneficial to balance social interactions intentionally. This involves recognizing personal thresholds for social stimulation and ensuring that they have adequate time for solitude and reflection to prevent feelings of being overwhelmed.

Creating environments that cater to introverted preferences, such as quiet spaces for focused work, allows introverts to leverage their strengths. These environments enable them to harness their abilities for concentration and deep thinking.

Rather than perceiving introversion as a hindrance, Cain's research encourages a perspective that acknowledges the unique strengths and contributions introverts bring to various settings, including the workplace and social interactions.

Holistic Strategies for Expanding Your Boundaries

Embarking on a journey of personal growth and expansion encompasses more than just breaking through individual barriers; it requires a holistic approach that nurtures the mind, body, and spirit.

More importantly, it is important to recognize that you do not need to cross any lines in order to evolve. Simply expanding your boundaries can help you lead a life of fulfillment.

That said, here are some useful strategies that can help you expand your limits:

Self-Acceptance

No matter where one stands or the challenges one faces, the journey to expand boundaries commences with a fundamental act: self-acceptance.

For people struggling with dyslexia, the initial step is to recognize dyslexia not as a limitation but as a unique aspect that contributes to a profound sense of self-acceptance. It involves acknowledging that dyslexia does not define one's worth or intelligence. Instead, it becomes a thread woven into the rich tapestry of individuality, bringing with it distinctive strengths, perspectives, and ways of thinking.

By fostering self-acceptance, individuals with dyslexia can liberate themselves from the shackles of societal expectations and stigmas. This self-awareness becomes the cornerstone upon which a journey of learning, adaptation, and growth can unfold. It paves the way for seeking support, implementing tailored strategies, and transforming perceived challenges into opportunities for development.

Similarly, for those who identify as introverted, the key lies in understanding and accepting introversion as a valid and valuable personality trait. Often, introverts may find themselves navigating a world that predominantly extols extroverted qualities. However, acknowledging introversion as a legitimate and potent aspect of one's character opens the door to a wealth of inherent strengths.

Introversion is not a deficiency but a distinctive way of engaging with the world. Deep thinking, reflective contemplation, and heightened empathy are among the many strengths associated with introversion. By recognizing and appreciating these qualities, individuals can navigate social dynamics with confidence and authenticity, embracing the power that introversion brings to personal and interpersonal spheres.

Take Courageous Initiatives

Initiating conversations, especially for those who are shy or introverted, can be a challenging yet transformative endeavor. So, it is important to choose settings where initiating conversations feels more comfortable. This could be during social events, workshops, or casual gatherings with familiar faces. Selecting approachable environments provides a supportive backdrop for taking the first step.

And while that first step outside your comfort zone may be difficult, it will lead to profound personal growth.

Begin with light, casual topics to ease into conversations. This could include commenting on the event, the surroundings, or common interests.

Maintain open and welcoming body language. Make eye contact, smile, and stand or sit in a way that conveys approachability.

Have a few conversation starters in mind before entering social situations. These could be related to recent events, shared interests, or general topics of discussion. Preparation provides a safety net and reduces anxiety associated with initiating conversations.

At the same time, it is important to establish specific, achievable goals for initiating conversations. This could involve setting a target for the number of conversations to start during an event. Setting specific yet achievable goals adds a structured approach to the process of initiating conversations. Whether it's aiming for a certain number of interactions during an event or initiating discussions with individuals of diverse backgrounds, these goals provide focus. Each accomplished goal becomes a milestone in expanding the comfort zone, fostering a sense of achievement.

Don't hesitate to reach out to friends or mentors for feedback and support. Actively reaching out to these trusted connections demonstrates a commitment to growth and a willingness to refine interpersonal skills. Consider scheduling regular check-ins or casual conversations to share your experiences and seek insights. When seeking feedback, be specific about the aspects you'd like input on, such as your communication style, conversational approach, or any particular challenges you've encountered.

But more than anything else, embrace the understanding that nobody is perfect. Every individual, regardless of their social prowess, makes mistakes and encounters moments of embarrassment. Accepting imperfections as part of the learning process is liberating. It allows for growth, resilience, and the development of a healthy perspective on the unpredictable nature of social interactions.

Practice Continuously

Cultivating a habit of continuous practice in social settings is a powerful strategy for individuals aiming to overcome shyness. The essence lies in regularly challenging oneself to step outside the familiar confines of the comfort zone and actively engage in conversations.

Besides, individuals who tend to be shy or introverted often possess commendable qualities such as politeness, intelligence, and knowledge, making them inherently insightful and intelligent. This self-awareness allows them to identify their limiting challenges, and remarkably, they possess the intelligence to navigate and overcome these obstacles strategically. Understanding that their strengths often outshine those of many others, these individuals have the unique ability to leverage their politeness, intelligence, and knowledge to their advantage.

Politeness fosters genuine connections, intelligence allows for meaningful contributions to conversations, and knowledge serves as a source of valuable insights. By reframing these qualities positively, individuals can cultivate a sense of self-worth and appreciate the distinctive strengths they bring to social interactions.

By consistently practicing, they can gradually expose themselves to therapy, desensitizing the fear associated with social interactions. It is much like building a muscle – the more you exercise it, the stronger it becomes. The repetitive nature of this practice reinforces positive communication habits, fostering a sense of ease and confidence over time.

But above all else, it is important to celebrate small victories. Acknowledge the progress made and reinforce the belief that you are capable of navigating social situations effectively. By doing so, you can make the process of continuous learning more effective and meaningful. Give yourself credit where it is due.

Brainstorming and Debating

For individuals who identify as shy or introverted, actively engaging in brainstorming and debating can be transformative in both personal and professional contexts.

If you fall in either of the categories, take the initiative to contribute your own ideas during brainstorming sessions. This practice will allow you to express thoughts and insights gradually.

It is important to set personal goals for each meeting, such as sharing one idea or perspective, which can create a manageable and measurable challenge. Simultaneously, participating in others' initiatives by offering constructive feedback or supporting their proposals fosters a collaborative environment.

But before you do, make sure you actively listen to what's being said. It is essential that you acknowledge the contributions of your peers before you voice your opinions.

If informal conversations seem too daunting, start with formal debates and discussions. Attempt to give your input where you feel the most comfortable. The key is to participate in initiatives actively, be it your own or someone else's. This practice helps you hone your communication skills and gain confidence.

Consistently practicing these actions not only enhances your own contributions but also strengthens your ability to navigate and thrive in group dynamics, gradually transcending the barriers of shyness or introversion. And once you master the art of formal brainstorming and debates, you can easily find yourself engaging in informal discussions with others.

Advocate for Yourself

Effective communication and self-advocacy are pivotal skills for individuals dealing with dyslexia.

But before that, develop a clear understanding of your unique needs. Whether it's related to dyslexia or any other challenge, identify specific areas where accommodations could enhance your ability to learn or work effectively. This might include extra time for reading, alternative assignment formats, or the use of assistive technologies.

Establish open lines of communication with teachers, employers, or peers. Share your experiences and challenges in a clear and constructive manner. Open communication fosters understanding and sets the stage for collaborative problem-solving.

Many people do not fully comprehend the nature of dyslexia or the specific accommodations that can be beneficial. Take the opportunity to educate teachers, employers, and peers about dyslexia, its impact on learning, and the types of support that can make a difference.

In educational settings, work with teachers and educational professionals to develop an Individualized Education Plan (IEP) or a similar accommodation plan. This document outlines specific accommodations tailored to your needs and ensures a structured and supportive learning environment.

Be assertive in expressing your needs and advocating for necessary accommodations. Clearly articulate how specific accommodations align with your learning or work style and contribute to your overall success.

Explore and incorporate assistive technologies that align with your needs. Screen readers, speech-to-text software, or dyslexia-friendly fonts are examples of tools that can enhance accessibility and support your learning or work objectives.

More importantly, develop and hone your self-advocacy skills over time. As you become more adept at articulating your needs and collaborating on solutions, you empower yourself to navigate diverse learning and work environments more effectively.

Develop Social Skills

Social skills are foundational for successful interactions in various aspects of life, from personal relationships to professional settings.

The good thing is anyone can develop social skills, whether they are dyslexic, introverted, or just shy.

Active listening is the first step to improving your social skills. It involves fully focusing, understanding, and responding to a speaker in a way that demonstrates genuine engagement. Practice giving your full attention during conversations and minimizing distractions. Use non-verbal cues, such as nodding or making appropriate facial expressions, to convey attentiveness. At the same time, don't be afraid to ask clarifying questions to delve deeper into the speaker's perspective.

Eye contact is another powerful non-verbal cue that signals attentiveness, sincerity, and connection. Practice making eye contact without staring. Aim for a natural and comfortable level. Use the 50/70 rule: maintain eye contact during at least 50% of the conversation when speaking and 70% when listening. If making direct eye contact is challenging, focus on looking at the area between the eyes.

The most important part is to actively engage in social situations to practice these skills. This can include both formal and informal settings. Observe individuals with strong social skills. Pay attention to how they listen, maintain eye contact, and express themselves.

In addition to honing interpersonal social skills, cultivating effective public speaking abilities is a valuable extension that enhances overall social competence.

To improve public speaking, start by organizing your thoughts coherently and structuring your message logically. Practice articulating your ideas with clarity and purpose.

Utilize vocal variety, such as tone and pace modulation, to keep your audience engaged. Pay attention to non-verbal cues, including gestures and body language, to convey confidence and authenticity.

Overcoming the fear of public speaking often involves gradual exposure, such as starting with smaller audiences and progressively working towards larger ones. Seek constructive feedback and learn from experienced speakers to refine your skills.

Take one step at a time. Eventually, you will start seeing your social limits expanding, allowing you to explore a wide range of social settings with confidence and ease.

Establish Boundaries

While it is good to work on your social skills and expand your boundaries, it is also equally important to thrive without pushing yourself too hard.

So, don't hesitate to establish some boundaries by understanding your own need for alone time. Recognize the signs of fatigue, stress, or the desire for solitude. This self-awareness forms the foundation for effective communication.

Foster open communication with friends and family members. Share your need for alone time transparently and explain its importance in maintaining your well-being. Clearly express how alone time contributes to your mental health, rejuvenation, and ability to engage more fully in social interactions when you reconnect.

In a work setting, communicate your need for focused, uninterrupted time for tasks or projects. Clearly express how this practice enhances your productivity and contributes to a positive work environment. If feasible, establish clear work hours to signal when you are available for collaboration and when you require dedicated focus.

Propose alternatives or compromises to assure others that your need for alone time does not hinder collaboration. This could include scheduling specific times for group activities or finding ways to reconnect after your period of solitude.

More than anything else, be consistent in practicing your established boundaries. This reinforces the reliability of your communication and builds trust with those around you. And while consistency is important, be adaptable when necessary. Flexibility in communication allows for adjustments based on evolving circumstances.

Choose Social Activities Wisely

For introverts, the landscape of social interactions can be both enriching and challenging. Engaging in social activities that align with personal interests and values is a strategic approach that allows introverts to balance their social lives effectively.

If you find yourself in a similar boat, begin by reflecting on your personal interests and values. What activities genuinely bring you joy, fulfillment, and a sense of connection? Understanding these elements lays the foundation for intentional social engagement.

Choose social activities that align with your identified interests. Whether it's joining a book club, participating in a hobby group, or attending events centered around your passions, purposeful selection ensures that your energy is invested in activities that resonate with you.

Introverts often thrive in meaningful, one-on-one or small group interactions. Prioritize forming deep connections over spreading yourself thin across numerous social events. Quality connections contribute more significantly to your well-being than a high quantity of superficial interactions.

Quality social interactions may be more energy-intensive for introverts. Factor in sufficient time for recharging after engaging in social activities. This time for solitude and reflection is essential to maintain a healthy balance.

More importantly, devote time to nurturing existing relationships rather than constantly seeking new ones. Deepening connections with a select few allows for a richer and more meaningful social experience.

Strategically plan downtime in your schedule. This allows you to recover and rejuvenate between social activities, ensuring that you can fully participate and enjoy each engagement.

At the same time, it is essential that you select social environments that align with your comfort level. Whether it's a cozy dinner with friends or a quiet gathering, choosing settings that resonate with your preferences enhances the overall quality of the experience.

Leverage Your Strengths

Many individuals with dyslexia possess a remarkable capacity for creative thinking. Dyslexic individuals often approach problems and tasks with a unique perspective, generating innovative ideas that others may not readily conceive. This heightened ability to visualize concepts and ideas can be a tremendous asset in fields such as art, design, architecture, and other creative pursuits.

So, actively challenge yourself to approach tasks or projects from unconventional angles. Encourage brainstorming sessions that embrace diverse perspectives. By consciously fostering out-of-the-box thinking, you infuse creativity and innovation into your work, fostering an environment that values diverse thought processes.

Embrace a mindset of continuous learning. Seek out opportunities to expand your knowledge and skills in areas that align with your interests. Continuous learning enhances your adaptability and keeps you at the forefront of developments in your chosen field.

Holistic growth involves an integrated approach, acknowledging the interconnectedness of various aspects of your life. By incorporating the strategies mentioned above into your routine, you can create a comprehensive and sustainable path for expanding your boundaries and embracing personal development regardless of your current social standing.

Chapter 3: Empowerment Within Bounds: Acknowledging Your Limits

The world is full of endless possibilities, and yet, some things remain out of reach. Every person has things they are good at and things they feel cannot be done. The circumstances of every individual vary. The important thing is to acknowledge your own limits. Start your journey by acknowledging the things you can and cannot do.

But that doesn't mean you stifle your ambitions. It just means you need a little bit of rerouting. Acknowledging your limits means starting at a point that is well within your boundaries. And then, you work on empowering yourself till you reach the end goal.

But what is empowerment?

It is an essential yet often overlooked aspect of life, particularly in marginalized communities. It refers to the process of gaining control over your own life, making informed decisions, and taking steps to better your circumstances.

Sounds simple enough, right? And yet, many individuals continue to navigate life without fully empowering themselves.

You see, empowerment is about recognizing your full potential and thriving within your boundaries. Ultimately, empowerment becomes the catalyst for change and personal growth.

That said, let's understand this concept with the help of a story:

Chelsea's Aspirations: A Journey of Success

Chelsea was a young woman living in Chicago, Illinois. Despite the vibrant energy of the city, Chelsea often felt constrained by the challenges life threw at her. Belonging to an immigrant family and being raised in a neighborhood marked by economic disparities and limited opportunities, Chelsea faced obstacles that seemed impossible to overcome.

Chelsea had dreams of pursuing higher education, specifically in psychology, but financial limitations forced her to take a different path. She found herself working long hours at a local diner, struggling to make ends meet. The constant grind made her acutely aware of her limitations.

In times like these, Chelsea chose to sketch out her frustrations. One day, while serving coffee to a group of artists, one of her drawings slipped from her pocket. One of the artists saw her work and was immediately impressed.

Listening to her mindless scribbles being praised was an eye-opening moment for Chelsea. She began to sketch during her breaks. To her surprise, the strokes of her pencil brought forth a world of creativity she never knew existed within her.

Acknowledging her artistic talent became a turning point for Chelsea. The act of creation became a refuge from the challenges that once held her back.

Ultimately, Chelsea joined a local initiative aimed at empowering individuals through art. This project, supported by the city's community development program, provided resources, mentorship, and a platform for artists from disadvantaged backgrounds.

Chelsea's artwork was unique and mesmerizing, immediately catching the attention of many art enthusiasts. Empowerment, in the form of recognition and support, became the catalyst for Chelsea's growth. The community rallied around her, providing opportunities for further education and exhibitions.

Eventually, Chelsea decided to revisit her original dream. With the support of her newfound community and scholarship opportunities, Chelsea enrolled in a local university to pursue her long-held aspiration of studying psychology.

As the doors of academia opened for her, Chelsea's journey became a testament to the limitless possibilities that unfold when one embraces one's strengths, overcomes obstacles, and seeks the empowering support of a community ready to uplift those who strive for more.

Significance of Acknowledged Limits and Empowerment

Recognizing and embracing limitations while simultaneously harnessing the intrinsic power to empower yourself are the capabilities that delve into the very essence of personal growth and resilience.

It helps create lines between ambition and realism. In doing so, individuals navigate the delicate balance of acknowledging their constraints, finding strength within bounds, and ultimately discovering the transformative force that leads to authentic empowerment.

Let's delve into the significance of acknowledged limits and empowerment by looking at some insightful research findings.

Decision-Making and Goal-Setting

Gollwitzer and Oettingen's research emphasizes the importance of setting goals that are both challenging and attainable.

Realistic goal-setting involves taking into account one's limitations, capabilities, and potential obstacles in the path to achievement. When individuals acknowledge their limits, they are better equipped to set goals that stretch their abilities without setting them up for inevitable failure.

Acknowledging limits involves a realistic assessment of personal constraints, whether they are related to time, resources, skills, or other factors. By understanding these constraints, individuals can make informed decisions about the types of goals that are feasible and align with their abilities. This understanding helps in crafting goals that are within reach and can be pursued with a higher likelihood of success.

Unrealistic expectations can lead to disappointment and demotivation. When individuals acknowledge their limits, they are less likely to set overly ambitious goals that may be unattainable. On the other hand, setting realistic expectations contributes to a more positive and sustainable approach to goal pursuit, enhancing the overall motivation to work towards achievable outcomes.

Achieving realistic goals fosters a sense of accomplishment. Gollwitzer and Oettingen's research highlights that individuals who set and attain realistic goals experience a positive feedback loop. Success in achieving manageable objectives boosts confidence and reinforces the belief that further goals are attainable. This sense of accomplishment becomes a powerful motivator for continued effort and goal pursuit.

Understanding one's limitations does not imply settling for mediocrity; rather, it encourages individuals to focus on meaningful and achievable objectives.

This realistic approach enhances intrinsic motivation, as individuals are more likely to stay committed and persistent when pursuing goals that align with their capabilities. The motivation to overcome challenges becomes more sustainable when individuals recognize and work within their limits.

Strength-Based Approach

Positive psychology, founded by Martin Seligman and Mihaly Csikszentmihalyi, seeks to understand and promote positive aspects of human experience, such as happiness, well-being, and personal strengths.

In their influential work "Positive Psychology: An Introduction," the researchers discuss the shift in focus from pathology and dysfunction to the exploration of positive aspects of human functioning.

The strengths-based approach encourages individuals to identify and recognize their inherent strengths, talents, and positive qualities. Rather than solely addressing and correcting weaknesses or deficits, this approach emphasizes the cultivation and application of what individuals are naturally good at.

The study suggests that when individuals intentionally use and apply their strengths in various aspects of their lives, they experience a boost in well-being. This may manifest as increased life satisfaction, a sense of accomplishment, and a higher overall quality of life.

Positive psychology interventions often involve activities aimed at helping individuals discover and utilize their strengths. These interventions may include exercises like strengths assessments, goal-setting based on strengths, and gratitude practices. Engaging in these activities is believed to enhance positive emotions and contribute to a more fulfilling life.

Csikszentmihalyi's concept of "flow" is closely related to this strengths-based approach. Flow is a state of optimal experience where individuals are fully engaged and immersed in an activity. When individuals align their strengths with their tasks, they are more likely to experience flow, leading to a heightened sense of enjoyment and accomplishment.

The researchers posit that by intentionally focusing on and utilizing one's strengths, individuals can cultivate a positive mindset and a greater sense of accomplishment. This, in turn, contributes to higher levels of well-being, resilience, and a more positive outlook on life.

Gender Empowerment

Naila Kabeer (2005) and Esther Duflo (2012) have made significant contributions to the understanding of gender empowerment and its impact on broader societal development goals. Their research underscores the multifaceted benefits of empowering women, particularly in the domains of education, health, and poverty reduction.

Kabeer's work emphasizes the pivotal role of gender empowerment in promoting women's access to education. When women are empowered, they are more likely to overcome social and economic barriers that hinder their educational opportunities. Empowered women tend to invest in their own education and that of their children, breaking the cycle of intergenerational poverty.

Both Kabeer and Duflo highlight the positive impact of gender empowerment on women's health outcomes. Empowered women are more likely to access healthcare services, make informed decisions about their reproductive health, and seek medical assistance when needed. This empowerment contributes to improved maternal and child health, reducing mortality rates and enhancing overall well-being.

Furthermore, empowering women plays a crucial role in poverty reduction efforts. Duflo's research, in particular, explores how women's economic empowerment can lead to broader economic development. When women have control over financial resources and decision-making, households and communities experience improved economic stability. This, in turn, contributes to the overall reduction of poverty at both individual and societal levels.

Both researchers emphasize the broader societal benefits of gender empowerment. When women are empowered, it positively influences social development indicators and contributes to greater gender equality. Empowered women are more likely to participate in decision-making processes at various levels, fostering inclusive and equitable societies.

Tips to Achieve Self-Empowerment

People only lend a helping hand to those who take the first step. And self-empowerment is all about taking that first step toward your goals.

However, striving for personal empowerment requires a conscious cultivation of internal drive and motivation. This innate desire serves as the catalyst for change, fueling the journey toward self-discovery and growth.

Identify what can be controlled, focus your energy and efforts on factors within your sphere of influence, and keep an objective, goal-oriented mindset.

That said, here are some useful tips that can help you achieve self-empowerment:

Cultivate a Positive Attitude

Cultivating a positive attitude is foundational to self-empowerment, as individuals who perceive themselves as architects of their destiny are more inclined to seize control of their future.

To develop this mindset, it is essential to break free from external notions of fate or luck and instead embrace the belief that one holds the reins of one's own life.

While it is true that some things remain beyond your limits, that doesn't mean you stop your efforts in achieving your goals. It simply means you need to carry out a thorough self-assessment.

Evaluate your strengths and weaknesses. This will become a pivotal step in the process of gaining control, allowing for a realistic self-assessment that identifies areas of potential growth and areas where existing strengths can be harnessed.

Engage in activities that genuinely interest and excite you. Pursuing passions not only brings joy but also fuels motivation, creating a positive and fulfilling environment.

However, at the same time, it is equally important to trust in your own abilities. A positive mindset is about acknowledging your past achievements, learning from your setbacks, and maintaining an optimistic perspective even when faced with adversities.

Instead of dwelling on setbacks, analyze them objectively, extract lessons, and use the experience to enhance resilience and problem-solving skills. Doing so will help you expand your limits and strive for even greater achievements.

Set Reasonable Goals

Setting measurable and achievable goals is crucial for self-empowerment, allowing individuals to track progress and experience a sense of accomplishment along the way.

Let's take an example where the goal is to run a marathon. The first step is to always define the goal, which, in this case, would be running a marathon.

Divide the marathon distance into smaller, achievable milestones. For instance, start with running a 5K (3.1 miles), then progress to a 10K (6.2 miles), half marathon (13.1 miles), and gradually build up to the full marathon distance.

Establish a realistic timeline for achieving each milestone. Consider your limits. In this case, these include factors such as your current fitness level, available time for training, and any other commitments.

Develop short-term goals for each phase of training. For instance, aim to run a certain distance or improve your pace within a specified time frame.

Implement gradual increases in distance and intensity to avoid overexertion and reduce the risk of injury. Incremental progress ensures that your body adapts gradually to the demands of running.

Regularly monitor your progress and be willing to adjust your goals based on your performance. At the same time, it is important to celebrate reaching each milestone. Acknowledging your achievements, no matter how small, boosts motivation and reinforces a positive mindset.

But don't forget that setting goals isn't only limited to marathons. It applies to every aspect of your life. Not only do goals empower you to achieve success, they also help you acknowledge your limits. Once you know where you stand, you can devise a strategy to reach the finish line by improving your capabilities.

Skill Enhancement

Identifying and enhancing skills relevant to your goals is a crucial step toward self-empowerment and personal development.

Start by clearly defining the skills that are essential for your goals. If you already possess these skills, work on improving them. Remember, no matter how good you are at something, there's always some room for improvement. This may involve taking courses, attending workshops, seeking mentorship, or engaging in practical experiences that allow you to apply and strengthen your skills.

For immigrants, language proficiency in the host country is often a critical factor. Assess your current language skills and identify areas for improvement. This could involve proficiency in speaking, reading, writing, and understanding both everyday and industry-specific language.

Consider the accessibility of skill development opportunities. Choose avenues that are within your reach in terms of time, finances, and location. Online courses, community resources, and local workshops can provide accessible options for skill enhancement.

Many host countries offer support services for immigrants, including language classes, vocational training, and mentorship programs. Take advantage of these services to enhance your skills, adapt to the new environment, and connect with the local community.

Language proficiency is not only about communication but also about cultural integration. Networking with native speakers, participating in community events, and immersing yourself in local culture can enhance your language skills and facilitate social integration.

More importantly, regularly assess your progress in skill development. Set measurable milestones to track improvement and make adjustments to your strategy as needed.

But skill enhancement isn't only limited to one particular group. It is a practice that is applicable to all. No matter what your end goal may be, the best way to realize your ambitions is by improving and expanding your skill set.

Build a Support System

Connecting with individuals who share similar backgrounds and experiences provides a unique understanding of the challenges you may face.

A supportive network can offer empathy and validation, acknowledging the unique struggles and triumphs associated with your identity or circumstances. This validation reinforces your sense of self-worth and resilience.

Supportive individuals can also provide encouragement and motivation during both successes and setbacks. Their belief in your abilities can boost your confidence, empowering you to overcome challenges and pursue your goals within your limits.

Whether you're a woman, disabled, or an immigrant, fellow women, immigrants, or individuals with disabilities may have practical advice and guidance based on their own experiences. This shared knowledge can help you navigate specific challenges more effectively, saving time and resources.

Besides, networks often involve resource sharing. Whether it's information, contacts, or opportunities, a supportive community is more likely to share resources that can benefit everyone involved, contributing to collective empowerment.

Being part of a supportive network fosters a sense of camaraderie and community. This connection can reduce feelings of isolation and create a space where you feel understood, accepted, and valued for who you are.

Campaigning and Lobbying

Last but not least, be sure to empower yourself by engaging in campaigns and lobbying. Doing so can be a potent change for influencing change and amplifying your voice. Remember, your efforts won't only empower you, but they also open doors for the community you represent.

Consider joining or initiating campaigns aligned with your values, whether they relate to social justice, equal rights, or community well-being.

Through lobbying efforts, you can directly communicate with policymakers and advocate for changes that matter to you. This involvement not only empowers you to make a meaningful impact on the world but also enhances your sense of agency and influence over your own destiny.

However, it is important to familiarize yourself with the ethical considerations and legal frameworks associated with lobbying. Understanding the rules ensures that your advocacy efforts adhere to ethical standards.

Explore and join existing campaigns led by reputable organizations. Collaborate with established groups to amplify your impact and benefit from collective knowledge and resources.

If you can't find any organizations, leverage social media platforms to raise awareness about your causes. Engage with online communities, share information, and encourage others to join your advocacy efforts.

At the end of the day, campaigning and lobbying will help you expand your internal and external limits, helping you lead a meaningful and fulfilling life.

Your boundaries are not your confines; embrace your limits and thrive within them. Do not let your gender, origin, or disability get in the way of your goals. Work on empowering yourself through a positive attitude, goal setting, skill enhancement, and your supportive network.

By incorporating the tips mentioned above, you can empower yourself to reach great heights.

Chapter 4: Professional Ethics and Client Relations

In the world of professional conduct, ethical considerations stand as the bedrock that upholds the integrity and trustworthiness of various occupations. Whether in healthcare, law, finance, or counseling, the significance of professional ethics cannot be overstated.

One pivotal facet of ethical practice involves a profound understanding of one's limits, particularly when it comes to client interactions. This awareness serves as a guiding principle to ensure that practitioners do not overstep boundaries and engage in actions that could prove inappropriate or illegal.

Upholding a standard of conduct that not only safeguards the interests of clients but also nurtures the essential trust between professionals and the individuals they serve.

In this context, the art of knowing one's limits becomes a key player, securing the delicate balance between providing effective services and steering clear of ethical pitfalls.

Let's understand this concept better with the help of a story.

Ethical Dilemma: Dr. Mitchell's Unveiling

Dr. Mitchell, a highly regarded psychologist practicing in San Francisco, California, had earned quite a reputation for his expertise in mental health and compassionate approach to therapy. His office was a sanctuary for clients seeking solace and guidance.

One day, a prominent tech executive named Ms. Davis sought Dr. Mitchell's psychological expertise. The initial sessions focused on managing workplace stress and achieving a healthier work-life balance. However, as trust developed, Mr. Davis began sharing personal struggles, including challenges in her marriage and family dynamics.

Soon, the two started meeting outside sessions. Dr. Mitchell unintentionally allowed the boundaries between therapist and confidante to blur. The therapeutic discussions shifted into increasingly personal topics, and a bond formed that surpassed the professional framework.

Word of their evolving relationship reached the board overseeing psychologists' ethical conduct. Concerns about the appropriateness of Dr. Mitchell's interactions with Ms. Davis reached her colleagues and the licensing board.

Consequences ensued swiftly. An investigation was initiated to scrutinize Dr. Mitchell's breach of professional ethics. The licensing board conducted interviews with both Dr. Mitchell and Ms. Davis, along with others privy to their interactions.

Ultimately, the board concluded that Dr. Mitchell had indeed crossed professional boundaries. The fallout was substantial—disciplinary actions were imposed, including a temporary suspension of Dr. Mitchell's license and mandatory participation in ethics training programs.

The repercussions extended beyond Dr. Mitchell's professional life. His reputation suffered, and the community he had served for years grappled with the revelation of a respected psychologist facing such consequences.

The ordeal taught Dr. Mitchell a very important lesson. No matter the client's vulnerability or the emotional connection that may arise, psychologists bear the responsibility of upholding ethical standards and maintaining professional boundaries with their clients.

Significance of Maintaining Ethical Boundaries with Clients

Maintaining professional limits with clients is a crucial aspect of ethical practice in various fields, including psychology, counseling, social work, and other helping professions.

The significance of establishing and adhering to these boundaries is well-documented in the research literature, as it contributes to the overall well-being of clients and ensures the integrity of the professional relationship.

Let's look at some insightful research findings that highlight the importance of maintaining ethical limits with clients.

Enhancing Trust and Safety

In Gabbard's work, the emphasis on clearly defined professional limits contributing to the development of trust and safety within the therapeutic relationship is rooted in psychodynamic principles and the dynamics of the therapeutic alliance.

Gabbard's perspective aligns with attachment theory, suggesting that a secure therapeutic relationship provides a "secure base" from which clients can explore their thoughts, emotions, and behaviors. Clearly defined professional limits create a structured and predictable environment similar to the secure base concept in attachment theory.

Clients often feel safer when they can predict the therapist's behavior and responses. Clearly defined professional limits contribute to a sense of consistency and predictability in the therapeutic relationship. This predictability helps clients feel more secure in the therapeutic setting.

Sharing sensitive information and discussing deep emotions can be challenging for clients. Gabbard's perspective suggests that when clients trust that their therapist maintains clear professional boundaries, they are more likely to feel emotionally safe. This emotional safety fosters a conducive environment for clients to open up without fear of judgment or inappropriate breaches of confidentiality.

Professional limits also include respecting clients' autonomy and personal space. When clients are assured that their therapist will not overstep these boundaries, it contributes to a sense of control and empowerment. This, in turn, enhances the trust between the client and therapist.

Gabbard and other psychodynamic theorists often highlight the importance of avoiding dual relationships, where therapists take on roles outside of the therapeutic setting. By maintaining clear professional limits, therapists avoid conflicts of interest and protect the integrity of the therapeutic relationship.

In psychodynamic therapy, transference and countertransference dynamics are also crucial elements. Clearly defined professional limits help manage these dynamics by providing a framework for understanding and addressing the emotions that may arise in the therapeutic relationship without compromising the therapeutic process.

Ethical and Legal Standards

The American Psychological Association (APA) provides an ethical framework for psychologists through its *Ethical Principles of Psychologists and Code of Conduct.* The ethical guidelines underscore the importance of maintaining professional limits and boundaries in the interactions between psychologists and their clients.

The primary concern of ethical guidelines is the welfare and protection of clients. Professional limits are established to ensure that psychologists provide competent and ethical services, avoiding any harm or exploitation of clients. This includes maintaining confidentiality, respecting autonomy, and avoiding dual relationships that could compromise the well-being of clients.

Professional limits are also crucial for maintaining the integrity of the therapeutic relationship. The APA's ethical guidelines emphasize the importance of objectivity and avoiding conflicts of interest. Psychologists are expected to establish and maintain clear and appropriate boundaries to ensure that the therapeutic relationship remains focused on the client's needs and goals.

The APA's ethical guidelines highlight the necessity of obtaining informed consent from clients. This includes clearly communicating the nature and limitations of the therapeutic relationship. Psychologists are required to inform clients about the boundaries of confidentiality, the goals of therapy, and the potential risks and benefits involved.

Violating professional limits can lead to the exploitation of clients, whether it involves financial, emotional, or personal exploitation. The ethical guidelines explicitly prohibit psychologists from engaging in any activities that may exploit clients or impair their professional judgment.

The APA's ethical guidelines serve as a standard for professional conduct, and psychologists are expected to adhere to these standards. Violating professional limits may result in legal and ethical consequences, including disciplinary actions, licensure revocation, and legal proceedings. These consequences are in place to maintain the public's trust in the profession and to ensure accountability.

Adhering to professional limits helps demonstrate the commitment of psychologists to ethical practice, which, in turn, fosters public confidence in the profession.

At the same time, it is important to remember that respecting professional limits is not only a requirement for ethical practice but also an essential aspect of ongoing professional development.

Promoting Objectivity

Maintaining professional limits is a key factor in promoting objectivity and preventing the intrusion of personal biases into client relationships. The work of Gerald Corey, Marianne Schneider Corey, and Patrick Callanan, particularly in their book "Issues and Ethics in the Helping Professions" (2018), emphasizes the importance of establishing and upholding these limits to ensure practitioners can provide effective and unbiased support to their clients.

Professional limits are essential in preventing countertransference, which refers to the therapist's emotional reactions to the client that are based on the therapist's own unresolved issues. By maintaining clear boundaries, therapists can reduce the likelihood of allowing their personal experiences and emotions to influence their understanding of the client's issues.

Professional limits contribute to the maintenance of neutrality, allowing practitioners to approach their clients with an open and unbiased mindset. This neutrality is crucial for accurately assessing the client's concerns, exploring various perspectives, and facilitating a therapeutic process free from undue influence.

Doing so also supports the autonomy of clients by ensuring that the focus remains on their needs and goals rather than the practitioner's personal agenda. This approach empowers clients to make their own decisions and choices, fostering a sense of independence and self-determination.

Besides, the establishment of professional boundaries is significant for avoiding confirmation bias, where practitioners might unconsciously seek or interpret information in a way that confirms their preexisting beliefs or assumptions. By maintaining boundaries, it is possible to approach each client with an open mind, free from preconceived notions.

More importantly, maintaining professional limits contributes to objectivity in the assessment and diagnosis of clients. By avoiding personal involvement or biases, practitioners can more accurately evaluate the client's presenting issues, leading to more effective treatment planning and intervention.

How to Maintain Professional Boundaries with Clients

Professional boundaries refer to the ethical and appropriate limits that define the scope and nature of the relationship between a professional and their clients, patients, or colleagues. These boundaries are established to ensure the well-being of the individuals involved, maintain professionalism, and uphold ethical standards.

In the professional world, navigating these limits without crossing the line is of utmost importance. One wrong step can land you in hot waters.

That said, here are some ways you can establish and maintain professional boundaries with clients, regardless of your profession:

Establish Clear Policies and Informed Consent

Communicate openly with clients, customers, or colleagues about the policies and guidelines that govern your professional interactions. Clearly articulate the expectations, rules, and norms associated with your professional role or service.

Clarify what information is considered confidential and the circumstances under which confidentiality may be breached. Transparency in communicating professional policies builds trust and sets clear expectations. It establishes a foundation for understanding the parameters within which the professional relationship will operate.

At the same time, it is important to highlight the legal and ethical boundaries within which your professional work operates. Clearly defining the nature and limitations of your professional role establishes clarity and trust. It helps prevent misunderstandings and ensures that all parties involved have a realistic understanding of what can be expected.

Moreover, you should define the purpose and objectives of your professional relationship or service. Make sure to outline your role and responsibilities, emphasizing how they align with the goals of the professional relationship.

More importantly, address potential conflicts of interest and explain how you navigate situations where dual roles might arise.

Moving toward informed consent, be sure to provide a comprehensive explanation of your professional approach, methods, and what clients, customers, or colleagues can expect from your services. Emphasize the voluntary nature of engagement and the right to discontinue the professional relationship or service.

Remember, obtaining informed consent is an ethical imperative that ensures individuals willingly engage in the professional relationship. It fosters a sense of autonomy and empowers individuals to make informed decisions about their participation.

Establish Clear Communication Channels

Using professional communication channels helps uphold a polished and credible image. It conveys a sense of professionalism and seriousness about the work. Use official email addresses, business communication platforms, or other designated channels established for work-related discussions.

Adhere to company policies and guidelines regarding information security. Avoid discussing confidential matters through personal emails or messaging apps. Remember, professional communication channels often have enhanced security measures to protect sensitive information. Using personal or informal methods may compromise the confidentiality and privacy of work-related discussions.

Keep a record of important discussions, decisions, and agreements made through professional communication channels. This documentation can serve as a reference point and reduce the risk of miscommunication.

At the same time, it is important to reserve personal communication methods for non-work-related interactions. Clearly communicate to clients or colleagues that professional discussions should occur through the established channels. This boundary is essential for preventing the intrusion of personal matters into the professional realm.

Besides, establishing designated communication channels sets clear expectations for how professional discussions should take place. It helps create a standardized and efficient communication process.

Use clear and concise language in professional communications. Avoid using ambiguous or informal language that may lead to misunderstandings.

Familiarize yourself with organizational communication policies and guidelines. Seek clarification if needed and align your communication practices accordingly. Adhering to these policies ensures compliance and avoids potential conflicts or violations.

Maintain Professional Demeanor

A professional demeanor helps ensure that interactions remain focused on the objectives and goals of the professional relationship. Avoid the unnecessary sharing of personal information to keep the conversation directed toward work-related matters. This promotes efficiency and effectiveness.

Make sure you only share relevant personal information with clients to maintain a polished and competent professional image. Doing so demonstrates a commitment to professionalism and enhances the perception of reliability and competence in the eyes of colleagues, clients, or superiors.

Besides, avoiding the unnecessary disclosure of personal details helps protect your privacy and personal boundaries. This is particularly important in online interactions, where information can be more easily disseminated and may have a lasting impact.

Personal information, if shared indiscriminately, may unintentionally introduce bias or prejudice into professional relationships. By keeping personal details relevant to the context, interactions can remain objective and free from unnecessary influences.

Make sure you adhere to the norms of communication, avoid gossip, and maintain a level of formality that is appropriate for the professional setting.

Remember, when personal boundaries are upheld, colleagues and clients are more likely to feel comfortable and respected.

Many organizations have policies in place regarding the sharing of personal information in professional contexts. Make sure to align with these policies to ensure compliance and avoid potential conflicts.

Respect Personal Space

Being mindful of physical boundaries communicates respect and consideration. This helps build trust and creates a comfortable atmosphere, making it more likely that individuals will feel at ease during professional interactions.

Pay attention to non-verbal cues, such as body language and facial expressions, to gauge the comfort level of others. Non-verbal cues provide valuable information about an individual's boundaries and comfort.

Encourage open communication about personal preferences regarding personal space. Creating a culture of open communication ensures that individuals feel comfortable expressing their boundaries.

More importantly, refrain from unnecessary physical contact such as hugs, pats on the back, or other gestures. Minimizing physical contact reinforces a professional and respectful atmosphere.

Instead, use professional greetings such as handshakes, nods, or verbal greetings that align with the cultural norms of the professional setting.

Be aware of and respect cultural differences regarding personal space. Set clear expectations for physical proximity during meetings or collaborative activities.

If inappropriate behavior occurs, address it promptly and according to organizational policies. Prompt resolution reinforces the commitment to maintaining a respectful and professional environment.

Demonstrate through your own behavior the importance of respecting personal space. Modeling appropriate behavior sets a standard for others to follow.

Be Mindful of Dual Relationships

A dual relationship occurs when a professional holds two different roles, such as a therapeutic and a personal role, with an individual. It can also refer to situations where the professional has multiple relationships with the same person, such as being both a colleague and a close friend.

Engaging in dual relationships can create conflicts of interest, where the professional's personal interests or relationships may conflict with their professional obligations. This conflict has the potential to compromise the objectivity and impartiality required in professional roles.

Dual relationships may pose a risk of impairing professional judgment. Personal connections can cloud objectivity and impact decision-making, leading to choices that are influenced by personal feelings rather than professional considerations.

In situations where dual relationships are unavoidable, informed consent and transparency become crucial. communicate openly about the dual roles, potential risks, and how you plan to manage any conflicts of interest.

However, it is important to note that engaging in certain types of dual relationships may have legal implications. For example, in therapeutic settings, some dual relationships could lead to allegations of professional misconduct or malpractice.

At the end of the day, you should always prioritize your professional role over personal relationships in situations where a conflict of interest may arise. Upholding the integrity of the professional role is crucial for maintaining trust and credibility.

Don't forget to educate clients or colleagues on the importance of maintaining professional boundaries and avoiding dual relationships. Transparent communication helps set expectations and prevents misunderstandings.

At the same time, you should stay informed about ethical guidelines and best practices through continuing education and training.

Set Boundaries for Gifts and Favors

Accepting gifts or favors can create a conflict of interest if it influences professional decision-making or compromises objectivity.

Professionals must make decisions based on merit and professional judgment. Accepting gifts may introduce bias and compromise the ability to remain objective. Communicate to clients, colleagues, or stakeholders your commitment to making decisions based on professional considerations rather than personal benefits.

Remember, accepting gifts, even innocently offered, may create a perception of indebtedness or influence. This perception can impact professional relationships and decisions. So, the best practice is to politely decline gifts that may pose a risk of influencing your professional conduct. Communicate your organization's gift policy to those you work with.

Some organizations set specific dollar limits for acceptable gifts to ensure transparency and prevent the acceptance of lavish or extravagant offerings. Advocate for or adhere to predetermined dollar limits established by your organization or professional association.

In situations where gift acceptance is unavoidable, transparency and disclosure are key. Communicate openly about received gifts and their nature.

Some situations may fall into gray areas. Establish a process for seeking guidance or making decisions in ambiguous cases. Consult with colleagues, supervisors, or an ethics committee when unsure about the appropriateness of accepting a gift.

By following the steps mentioned above, professionals in various fields can create and maintain appropriate boundaries with clients, fostering a healthy and ethical working relationship. The goal is to ensure professionalism, integrity, and trust while upholding ethical standards in the workplace.

Chapter 5: Navigating Technology and Digital Boundaries

In today's digital and interconnected world, maintaining boundaries is essential to safeguard personal privacy, mental well-being, and overall security.

As technology continues to permeate every aspect of life, establishing clear boundaries helps prevent the erosion of privacy by regulating the extent to which personal information is shared online. Setting limits on screen time and digital interactions is essential for preserving mental health, reducing the risk of addiction, and fostering meaningful face-to-face connections.

Additionally, maintaining boundaries with technology is vital for protecting oneself from cyber threats, such as identity theft and online harassment.

By being mindful of the impact of technology on everyday life and consciously establishing limits, individuals can strike a balance between the benefits and potential drawbacks of the digital age, promoting a healthier and more secure online existence.

That said, let's understand the significance of establishing and maintaining digital boundaries with the help of a story.

Unplugged in the City: Rebecca Navigates Digital Boundaries

Rebecca was a young high school student in New York. Living in such a bustling city, she constantly found herself immersed in the fast-paced world, not only physically but also digitally. Her life became a constant stream of social media updates, notifications, and online comparisons.

Rebecca was unable to establish clear digital boundaries, often spending hours mindlessly scrolling through social media platforms. She began measuring her self-worth against the seemingly perfect lives depicted by others, fueling a sense of inadequacy.

As Rebecca's dependence on social media grew, she found herself constantly seeking validation through likes and comments. The continuous exposure to curated content and idealized lifestyles took a toll on her mental health. Anxiety and self-doubt crept in, impacting her real-world relationships and work performance. The blurred lines between her online and offline existence left Rebecca feeling overwhelmed and isolated.

It wasn't until a breaking point, marked by a particularly harsh comment on one of her posts about her appearance, that Rebecca realized the detrimental effects of her lack of digital boundaries. The comment was a stark example of the negativity that can thrive on social media platforms.

Ultimately, Rebecca decided to take a step back, reassess her priorities, and set limits on her social media use. Seeking support from friends, family, and even professional counseling, Rebecca gradually reclaimed control over her life.

Through this experience, Rebecca learned the importance of respecting digital boundaries for mental well-being. She discovered that a healthy balance between the digital and physical worlds was essential for a fulfilling life.

The lesson she took away resonates as a reminder for others to be mindful of the impact of technology on their mental health and to establish boundaries that foster a positive and balanced lifestyle.

Impact of Technology on Mental Health and Privacy

In an era defined by the omnipresence of digital technologies, the intricate relationship between technology, mental health, and privacy has become a subject of intense scrutiny.

The convergence of personal lives with the digital world has ushered in both unparalleled conveniences and complex challenges.

As individuals increasingly find themselves navigating the digital landscape, researchers have delved into the multifaceted impact of technology on mental well-being and privacy.

Let's explore the impact of technology on everyday life with the help of insightful research findings.

Mental Health

The study conducted by Twenge, J. M., and Campbell, W. K. in 2018 investigated the potential link between excessive technology use, specifically social media engagement, and adverse mental health outcomes, with a particular focus on young adults in the United States. The research aimed to discern any patterns or associations between the rise of social media use and mental health trends over an eight-year period spanning from 2009 to 2017.

The findings of the study were particularly noteworthy, revealing a significant increase in major depressive episodes and suicidal thoughts among the demographic of young adults during the specified timeframe. Importantly, this concerning trend coincided temporally with the surge in social media usage. The implication is that the heightened prevalence of these mental health challenges observed in the study could be correlated with the propagation of social media platforms.

One plausible interpretation of these results is that the constant exposure to social media, with its curated depictions of idealized lifestyles and the pervasive culture of comparison, may contribute to the development or exacerbation of mental health issues.

The study highlights the importance of recognizing the potential impact of digital technologies, specifically social media, on the psychological well-being of young adults. It underscores the need for further research and increased awareness to inform strategies for promoting a healthy and balanced relationship between individuals and the digital landscape in the evolving context of the 21st century.

Privacy

The research conducted by Buchanan, T., Paine, C., Joinson, A. N., & Reips, U. in 2007 delved into the critical issue of privacy in the digital age, specifically exploring how technology, particularly social media platforms, influences individuals' perceptions and behaviors regarding personal information security.

The study aimed to shed light on the complex interplay between user attitudes, behaviors, and the actual risks associated with sharing personal information online.

One of the key revelations from the investigation was the tendency of individuals to underestimate the privacy risks linked to divulging personal information on social media platforms.

In the world of social media, users often engage in sharing various aspects of their lives, from personal preferences to detailed life events, under the assumption that the platforms provide a secure environment. However, the study brought to light the inherent discrepancies between users' perceptions and the actual privacy risks present in the digital landscape.

The implications of this finding are significant. The underestimation of privacy risks can render individuals more susceptible to potential vulnerabilities, such as identity theft, unauthorized access to personal information, or even online harassment. This disparity between perceived and actual risks underscores the need for enhanced digital literacy and education to empower individuals to make informed decisions about what they share online and understand the potential consequences.

As technology continues to evolve and digital interactions become more ingrained in daily life, studies like this serve as important indicators of the challenges individuals face in maintaining control over their personal information.

It emphasizes the urgency for both users and technology platforms to prioritize privacy awareness, implement robust security measures, and foster a culture that promotes responsible and informed online behaviors.

Positive Impact

The study conducted by Joseph et al. in 2017 represents a significant contribution to the growing body of research exploring the positive impact of technology on mental health. This particular investigation focused on the effectiveness of mental health apps as tools for therapy and support, with a specific emphasis on their role in mitigating symptoms of depression and anxiety.

The findings of the study underscored the potential of technology to serve as a valuable resource in mental health improvement. By assessing the impact of mental health apps, the research aimed to determine whether these digital tools could offer meaningful support and intervention for individuals experiencing symptoms of depression and anxiety.

One notable aspect of the study was the positive correlation identified between the use of mental health apps and a reduction in symptoms.

The results suggested that individuals engaging with these apps experienced tangible benefits, indicating that technology could play a pivotal role in providing accessible and effective mental health support. This is particularly relevant given the widespread accessibility of smartphones and the potential to reach diverse demographics with digital interventions.

The implications of this research are profound, highlighting how technology can be harnessed as a tool for mental health improvement, especially in the context of conditions like depression and anxiety.

Mental health apps offer convenience, anonymity, and personalized approaches to support, making them accessible to individuals who might face barriers to traditional forms of therapy.

While acknowledging the positive impact of technology on mental health, it's crucial to maintain a balanced perspective, recognizing that the same digital tools can contribute to challenges when not used mindfully.

Tips for Navigating Digital Boundaries

In an age dominated by digital connectivity, mastering the art of navigating digital boundaries has become a cornerstone of maintaining a balanced and fulfilling life.

As technology continues to weave its way into every facet of life, from personal relationships to work responsibilities, the need to establish clear limits and cultivate a healthy relationship with digital devices has never been more critical.

This journey is one that requires self-awareness, intentionality, and a conscious effort to strike a harmonious balance between the benefits and potential pitfalls of our interconnected world.

That said, here are some tips for navigating the intricacies of digital boundaries:

Set Clear Limits
Setting clear limits on your digital device usage is a foundational step in establishing healthy boundaries.

Begin by assessing your current digital habits. Take note of the apps or activities that consume a significant portion of your time. Once you've identified them, set specific and realistic time limits for each.

For instance, if you find yourself spending excessive time on social media, decide on a daily limit for scrolling or designate specific periods during the day for such activities. Utilize the built-in screen time tracking features on smartphones or consider third-party apps that help you monitor and control your usage.

Create a schedule that reflects your digital boundaries. Allocate time blocks for work-related digital tasks, leisure, and essential functions like communication. Stick to this schedule as closely as possible to ensure a disciplined approach to your digital consumption.

Consider implementing "no-tech" zones or times, such as during meals, an hour before bedtime, or when engaging in activities with family and friends. This intentional disconnection allows for mental recharge and fosters a healthier balance between your online and offline life.

Regularly assess your progress and be flexible in adjusting your limits based on evolving needs and circumstances. The key is to strike a balance that aligns with your lifestyle and promotes overall well-being.

Remember, the goal is not to eliminate digital interactions but to cultivate a conscious and intentional relationship with technology. By setting clear limits, you empower yourself to use digital devices as tools for productivity and enjoyment without succumbing to the pitfalls of mindless scrolling or overconsumption.

Manage Notifications

Controlling your device notifications is a strategic move to regain focus and reduce the constant stream of digital interruptions.

Take a moment to identify the notifications that are truly essential for your daily functioning, such as messages from important contacts, work-related updates, or urgent reminders. This step helps distinguish crucial alerts from non-essential ones.

Navigate to the notification settings on your device, which can typically be found in the system settings or through the individual settings of each app. Explore the customization options available for different types of notifications.

Disable notifications for apps or categories that contribute to unnecessary distractions. This might include social media updates, promotional emails, or non-urgent news alerts. Be selective in retaining only those notifications that are directly relevant to your priorities.

Don't forget to take advantage of the "Do Not Disturb" mode during specific periods when you need concentrated focus, such as during work hours or when engaging in important tasks. Customize this mode to allow notifications from essential contacts or apps while silencing the rest.

Audit Your Digital Presence

Auditing your digital presence involves a proactive review of the information you share online and the settings that govern your privacy.

Develop a checklist of privacy considerations for your social media accounts. Include items such as profile information, post visibility, friend or follower requests, and connected apps. This checklist will serve as a guide during your audit.

Start by reviewing the information on your social media profiles. Ensure that details such as your bio, location, and contact information are up-to-date. Consider whether you want this information to be visible to the public or restricted to a select audience.

Examine the default visibility settings for your posts. Social media platforms often allow you to customize who can see your content. Adjust these settings based on your comfort level and the nature of the information you're sharing. For more sensitive content, limit visibility to trusted friends or connections.

Assess your friend or follower lists. Remove or unfollow accounts that are no longer relevant or pose privacy concerns. Be discerning about accepting new requests, ensuring that your online connections align with your personal boundaries.

At the same time, it is important to audit the third-party apps connected to your social media accounts. Review the permissions granted to these apps and consider revoking access for those that no longer serve a purpose or may compromise your privacy. Be cautious about granting unnecessary permissions.

Digital Detox Days

Implementing digital detox days involves intentionally disconnecting from screens to rejuvenate your mental and physical well-being.

Schedule digital detox days in advance, considering your work commitments and personal schedule. Choose a frequency that is realistic for you, whether it's once a week, bi-weekly, or on a monthly basis.

Inform friends, family, and colleagues about your digital detox day, setting clear expectations that you won't be readily available through digital channels. This helps manage expectations and reduces the likelihood of urgent messages.

Establish specific rules for your digital detox day. This may include refraining from checking emails, social media, or any non-essential digital communication. Clearly define what qualifies as a digital activity and commit to abstaining from these during the detox period.

Plan outdoor activities that don't involve screens. This could be a nature walk, hiking, biking, or simply spending time in a local park. Connecting with nature and engaging in physical activities can provide a refreshing break from screen-related stressors.

If you wish to read, choose a book in print and dedicate time to immerse yourself in its pages. Reading a physical book not only eliminates screen exposure but also promotes focused and uninterrupted deep reading, fostering mental relaxation.

Prioritize Real-Life Connections

Prioritizing real-life connections involves consciously choosing face-to-face interactions over digital communication to enhance emotional well-being and mitigate the potential isolation associated with excessive technology use.

Actively plan and schedule face-to-face meetings with friends, family, and colleagues. This could be casual outings, meals, or structured events. Regular in-person interactions strengthen bonds and provide a richer emotional experience compared to digital communication.

Participate in group activities or events that facilitate real-life connections. Whether it's joining a club, attending local meetups, or participating in community events, group activities offer opportunities for meaningful face-to-face engagement.

When spending time with others, designate specific periods as tech-free. Put away phones and other devices to fully engage in the present moment. This not only enhances the quality of interactions but also reduces distractions.

While digital communication is convenient for planning, try to limit it to logistical aspects. Save meaningful conversations and updates for face-to-face interactions, allowing for deeper and more nuanced connections.

Remember that finding the right balance is a personal journey, and it may take time to develop habits that work best for you. Regularly reassess and adjust your digital boundaries based on your evolving needs and priorities.

Chapter 6: Competence and Qualifications

Competence and qualification are vital in professional and personal domains, serving as cornerstones for effective performance and success.

Competence reflects one's ability to navigate tasks and responsibilities adeptly, ensuring that undertakings are executed with skill and precision. Qualifications, on the other hand, signify the attainment of a certain level of education, training, or experience in a specific field.

Adhering to the boundaries set by one's competence and qualifications is crucial as it guarantees a solid foundation for decision-making and task execution. When individuals operate within their established limits, they are more likely to achieve optimal results, fostering a culture of expertise, reliability, and ethical conduct.

Crossing these boundaries can lead to suboptimal outcomes, jeopardizing the quality of work, integrity, and trust in personal and professional relationships. Thus, recognizing and respecting these limits is essential for sustained success and the maintenance of ethical standards.

Let's understand the significance of staying within one's limits with the help of a story:

A Well-Intentioned Misstep: Dr. Morgan Crosses the Line

Dr. Morgan was a highly respected cardiologist renowned for his expertise in heart health. One day, he found himself facing an unexpected challenge.

After successfully treating Mr. Johnson, a patient who had suffered a heart attack, Dr. Morgan continued to provide guidance during the follow-up appointments. However, when Mr. Johnson began experiencing persistent headaches, Dr. Morgan, wanting to address all his patient's concerns, inadvertently stepped outside the world of cardiology.

Despite his lack of qualifications in neurology, Dr. Morgan, driven by a genuine desire to help, offered advice on potential causes for the headaches and recommended a course of action.

Unfortunately, Mr. Johnson's condition did not improve and, in fact, worsened over time. Concerned about the unexpected turn of events, Mr. Johnson sought the expertise of a neurologist, who identified an underlying neurological issue that required immediate attention.

News of the incident reached the state medical board, leading to an investigation into Dr. Morgan's actions. It became clear that his intentions were rooted in a sincere commitment to his patient's well-being, but the consequences of advising beyond his field of expertise were significant. Dr. Morgan faced disciplinary action and a dent in his once-pristine professional reputation.

This incident served as a poignant reminder within the medical community about the critical importance of staying within the bounds of one's competence and qualifications, especially when it comes to comprehensive patient care.

Humbled by the experience, Dr. Morgan publicly acknowledged his error and committed to reinforcing the principles of ethical medical practice in his future interactions with patients.

The Consequences of Professional Malpractice and Negligence

Negligence and malpractice can have serious consequences across various professions, impacting individuals' well-being, public trust, and the overall integrity of professional fields.

That said, let's understand these consequences by looking at some insightful research findings:

Sanctions

The study by Blendon et al. suggests that both the public and a significant portion of physicians support the use of sanctions against individual health professionals perceived as responsible for serious errors. This finding highlights the importance of accountability and consequences for medical professionals in cases of severe negligence or malpractice.

The public's support for sanctions against health professionals indicates a strong societal expectation for accountability within the healthcare system. When errors or malpractice occur, individuals often look for measures that hold responsible parties accountable to maintain trust in the healthcare profession.

The fact that physicians themselves support the use of sanctions underscores a commitment within the medical community to uphold high standards of care. This internal acknowledgment emphasizes the importance of self-regulation and a collective responsibility to maintain the integrity of the medical profession.

The study's findings suggest that sanctions are viewed not just as punitive measures but as essential tools for rebuilding and maintaining trust in the healthcare system.

Knowing that both the public and fellow professionals support sanctions may serve as a deterrent for medical professionals, encouraging adherence to best practices and ethical standards.

The threat of sanctions can act as a preventive measure, potentially reducing the likelihood of serious errors or negligence.

The study's results have potential implications for healthcare policies and regulations. If there is widespread support for sanctions, policymakers may be more inclined to implement or strengthen measures that hold health professionals accountable for their actions. This can include legal consequences, professional sanctions, or other disciplinary actions.

While sanctions are crucial for accountability, it's important to strike a balance that also promotes a culture of learning and continuous improvement within the medical field. Identifying and addressing the root causes of errors, rather than solely focusing on punitive measures, can contribute to overall system improvement.

Impact on Patient Safety and Trust

Negligence or malpractice in the field of medicine can have profound and far-reaching consequences that impact patients, erode trust in healthcare providers, and initiate legal repercussions.

The pivotal study conducted by Brennan et al. in 1991 stands as a landmark investigation revealing the extent of adverse events associated with medical negligence among hospitalized patients.

The study delved into the occurrence of adverse events, which encompassed instances where patient harm resulted from medical care and negligence, indicating a departure from the standard of care expected from healthcare professionals. The findings of the study underscored the alarming prevalence of adverse events linked to medical negligence within hospital settings.

One of the key takeaways from the study was the acknowledgment of a substantial number of patients experiencing harm due to medical errors or negligence during their hospital stays. This revelation illuminated the urgent need for advancements in patient safety protocols, emphasizing the critical importance of preventing, identifying, and rectifying instances of medical malpractice.

The consequences of medical negligence, as highlighted by the study, include the direct harm inflicted upon patients, ranging from physical injuries to exacerbated health conditions. Moreover, the erosion of trust in healthcare providers is a significant collateral effect, as patients and the broader public rely on medical professionals for their expertise, care, and commitment to ethical standards.

Legal ramifications further compound the aftermath of medical negligence, with patients seeking justice and compensation for the harm they have endured. The legal dimension emphasizes the accountability of healthcare providers and institutions, emphasizing the societal expectation for transparency, responsibility, and continuous improvement within the healthcare system.

Reputational Damage

Negligence or malpractice in the legal field can have profound consequences, impacting not only the financial well-being of clients but also the outcome of legal cases and the reputation of legal professionals.

The research conducted by Merry, Sally & Silbey, Susan in 1984 delves into client expectations and dissatisfaction with legal representation, providing valuable insights into the potential repercussions of malpractice in the legal profession.

One of the immediate and tangible outcomes of legal malpractice is financial loss for the client. Legal representation comes with costs, and if negligence occurs, it may lead to adverse financial consequences for the client, including loss of funds spent on legal fees, settlements, or potential damages that could have been avoided with competent representation.

Legal malpractice can significantly compromise the client's case, affecting the outcome and potentially leading to unfavorable rulings. Errors in legal strategy, failure to meet deadlines, or inadequate representation can result in weakened legal positions, negatively impacting the client's chances of success in litigation.

The research highlights the importance of understanding client expectations in legal representation. When legal professionals fail to meet these expectations due to negligence, it can lead to dissatisfaction and erosion of trust. Clients rely on their attorneys not only for legal expertise but also for effective communication, transparency, and diligent representation.

Legal malpractice can harm the reputation of individual attorneys and law firms. Word-of-mouth and reviews from dissatisfied clients can spread, potentially impacting the ability of legal professionals to attract new clients and maintain a positive professional standing within the legal community.

Legal malpractice may also have ethical and professional consequences for attorneys. Depending on the severity of the negligence, legal professionals may face disciplinary actions, including censure, suspension, or disbarment. This not only affects individual careers but serves as a deterrent for maintaining ethical standards within the legal profession.

Learning to Stay Within Your Area of Expertise

Navigating the professional landscape requires a delicate balance between embracing opportunities for growth and staying within the boundaries of one's expertise.

In a world that values versatility and adaptability, professionals often find themselves at the crossroads of expanding their skill set and ensuring a steadfast commitment to their established areas of expertise.

However, this expansion demands a nuanced approach – one that encourages continuous learning while guarding against the pitfalls of overreach.

Here are some tips that can help you expand your limits respectfully without wondering past your area of expertise:

Recognize Your Limits

Clear self-awareness of your knowledge, skills, and experience is fundamental for navigating personal and professional endeavors effectively.

It involves a candid and honest evaluation of your capabilities, delineating what falls within your expertise and recognizing the areas that lie outside of it. This recognition of limits is a crucial first step in avoiding overreach and potential pitfalls.

By acknowledging the boundaries of your proficiency, you gain a realistic understanding of your strengths and weaknesses.

Start by clearly defining your core competencies – the specific skills and knowledge that form the backbone of your expertise. Focus on the areas where you have a deep understanding and a history of successful application. This clarity helps in setting boundaries.

If your expertise spans multiple domains, identify the specialized areas within each domain where you possess in-depth knowledge.

Engage with peers, colleagues, or mentors to gain external perspectives on your strengths and areas of expertise. Constructive feedback from those who have observed your work can offer valuable insights and confirm your self-assessment.

But more than anything else, stay informed about the areas that are out of your reach. While it is important to work on improving yourself and acquiring new skills, it is equally paramount to be aware of where you may lack competence or qualification to avoid instances of malpractice.

Stay Up to Date

Stay updated within your field of expertise. Regularly read industry publications, journals, and reputable online platforms related to your field. Subscribe to newsletters and set aside dedicated time to stay informed about the latest research, trends, and developments.

Make learning a consistent part of your routine by allocating dedicated time each week to stay updated. Treat it as an essential professional responsibility, and integrate it into your schedule to ensure continuous growth and relevance in your field. Doing so not only enhances your competence but also positions you as a knowledgeable and adaptable professional in an ever-evolving work environment.

You can always become a member of professional associations relevant to your expertise. Attend conferences, seminars, and networking events organized by these associations.
Membership often includes access to exclusive resources and insights that can help you stay at the forefront of your field.

At the same time, it is important to actively engage in professional networking both online and offline. Connect with peers, attend industry meetups, and participate in forums or discussion groups. Networking provides opportunities to share knowledge, discuss industry trends, and learn from others' experiences.

Collaborate with Experts

When a task or project falls outside your domain of expertise, you should always opt for collaboration. Be honest with yourself about your limitations, and avoid attempting to tackle something that falls outside your skill set.

Once you've recognized the need for specialized knowledge, identify experts in the specific area related to the project or task. Look for professionals with a proven track record, expertise, and experience in the domain you need assistance with.

Take the initiative to reach out to the identified experts. Initiate a conversation to discuss the project, explain your goals, and express your interest in collaboration. Clear communication is key to establishing a collaborative partnership.

Clearly articulate your strengths and the aspects of the project that align with your expertise. Simultaneously, be transparent about the specific areas where you need assistance. This honesty lays the foundation for a collaborative relationship built on mutual understanding.

More importantly, create an environment that encourages knowledge sharing. Foster open communication where ideas, insights, and expertise can be freely exchanged. This not only enhances the quality of the current collaboration but also sets the stage for potential future collaborations.

Clearly Define the Scope of Work

When taking on projects or tasks, clearly define the scope of work.

Begin each project or task with a comprehensive kickoff meeting or communication. This is an opportunity to discuss project goals, objectives, and expectations. Clearly outline your role and the specific areas where your expertise will be applied.

Develop a detailed project scope document that outlines the specific tasks, milestones, and deliverables. Clearly articulate what falls within the scope of your responsibilities and what might be outside the defined boundaries. Share this document with all relevant stakeholders.

Communicate any limitations or constraints that may affect the project. If there are areas where you may not have expertise or where external input is required, make these points clear upfront. Transparency about potential challenges helps manage expectations.

Throughout the project, seek feedback and confirmation from clients or team members. Ensure that they are satisfied with the work completed and that it aligns with their expectations. Address any concerns promptly to maintain a positive working relationship and avoid any unintended consequences afterward.

At the same time, it is important to be comfortable saying "no" to opportunities or projects that fall outside your area of expertise. It's better to decline and maintain your credibility than to take on something you're not equipped to handle.

Evaluate Risks and Consequences

Before venturing into new areas, evaluate the potential risks and consequences. Identify potential challenges, uncertainties, and obstacles that may arise. This assessment should encompass both internal factors (such as your current skill set and resources) and external factors (such as market trends or competition).

Align any new ventures with your long-term professional goals. Evaluate how the proposed endeavor contributes to your overall career trajectory. Consider whether it enhances your skill set, aligns with your aspirations, or opens up opportunities that align with your broader professional objectives.

Identify any skill or knowledge gaps that may exist in the new area you're considering. Understanding the necessary competencies helps you gauge your preparedness for the venture. If you feel you lack the competency or qualification needed, it is important to first work on these areas beforehand.

Clearly define the potential benefits of venturing into the new area. This may include professional growth, expanded opportunities, increased revenue, or other positive outcomes. Quantify these benefits where possible to make a more informed decision.

By adhering to the tips mentioned above, you can maintain a strong focus on your area of expertise, deliver high-quality work, and build a reputation as a reliable and knowledgeable professional.

Remember, there may be times when certain tasks or projects might seem tempting, but if they fall outside your boundaries, it is best to say no or work on yourself till you reach the level of competency and qualification needed for execution.

Chapter 7: Authority and Jurisdiction

The concepts of authority and jurisdiction play important roles in maintaining order and fostering the well-being of communities.

Authority, often synonymous with power, refers to the legitimate right to exercise control and make decisions. On the other hand, jurisdiction defines the boundaries within which this authority is applied.

The convergence of authority and jurisdiction highlights a delicate balance that individuals in positions of power must navigate. While possessing authority provides the means to effect change and bring about positive outcomes, the misuse or overstepping of such power can have profound consequences.

This delicate interplay between authority and jurisdiction necessitates a responsible approach, emphasizing the importance of staying within prescribed boundaries and employing one's influence for the greater good.

That said, let's understand the significance of understanding your limits in the context of authority and jurisdiction with the help of a story.

Breach of Trust: Vivian's Downfall

Vivian was a high-ranking official holding a position of considerable authority within the local government. She was entrusted with making decisions that affected the lives of countless citizens.

Despite the weight of her responsibilities, Vivian harbored ambitions that exceeded the bounds of her official jurisdiction. Fueled by a desire for personal gain, she devised a scheme to exploit her position for financial advantage.

Under the guise of a civic improvement project, Vivian diverted public funds to a private venture, lining her pockets while neglecting the pressing needs of the community.

As whispers of corruption and misuse of public resources circulated, a vigilant investigative journalist named Alex took up the challenge of exposing the truth. Through meticulous research and courageous reporting, Alex unveiled the extent of Vivian's transgressions, shaking the foundations of trust that the citizens had placed in their officials.

In the wake of the scandal, legal authorities initiated a thorough investigation into Vivian's actions. The evidence was concrete, and it became clear that she had overstepped her authority in pursuit of personal gain.

As the legal proceedings unfolded, Vivian faced a reckoning. The courtroom drama captivated the city, with citizens closely following the trial as justice sought to hold the errant official accountable for her actions. Ultimately, a decision was made, and the court ruled against Vivian, finding her guilty of corruption, misuse of public funds, and a breach of the public trust.

The consequences were swift and severe. Vivian was stripped of her position, and the ill-gotten gains were confiscated to be returned to the community she had betrayed. The legal ramifications echoed beyond the individual, serving as a stern warning to those who might be tempted to abuse their authority for personal gain.

Consequences of Stepping Outside Authority and Jurisdiction

Stepping outside the established bounds of authority and jurisdiction can have profound consequences that resonate across legal, organizational, and ethical dimensions.

The repercussions of overstepping these boundaries extend beyond individual actions, impacting entire systems, organizations, and, in some cases, international relations.

As individuals or entities venture beyond their prescribed limits, they risk legal liabilities, organizational turmoil, and ethical dilemmas that can erode trust and stability.

That said, let's understand the consequences of overstepping authority and jurisdiction by looking at some insightful research findings.

Economic Decline

In their seminal work in 1998, Kaufmann and Gray highlighted the detrimental and far-reaching consequences of bribery on economic outcomes. Their research emphasized that beyond the immediate ethical concerns associated with bribery, its impact resonates in both foreign and domestic spheres, resulting in ineffective economic results and hindering the potential for sustainable growth.

The research pointed out that bribery causes economic inefficiency by diverting resources away from productive uses. The allocation of investments becomes distorted, with a preference for projects that might yield immediate gains through bribery, such as major defense or unnecessary infrastructure projects. This not only undermines the potential for economic growth but also obstructs the development of critical sectors, such as healthcare, as investments are diverted away from essential areas like rural specialist health clinics and preventive healthcare.

The study underscores how bribery distorts the allocation of talent within a society. The lure of illicit gains through bribery can divert skilled individuals from sectors that contribute to societal well-being toward areas where corruption yields quicker returns. This impedes not only human capital development but also skews sectorial priorities and technology choices, perpetuating a cycle of inefficiency and hindering long-term economic sustainability.

One of the notable consequences highlighted by Kaufmann and Gray is the tendency for bribery to drive economic activities into the "underground" or informal sector. This not only diminishes the state's ability to regulate and collect taxes but also weakens institutions responsible for maintaining the rule of law.

As economic activities move beyond the formal sector, the state struggles to generate sufficient revenue, leading to increased tax rates imposed on a shrinking base of taxpayers.

Erosion of Trust and Legitimacy

Public trust in institutions is a cornerstone of a well-functioning society, underpinning the legitimacy and effectiveness of governmental bodies and officials. However, when individuals or entities overstep their authority, the delicate fabric of trust between the public and these institutions can unravel.

The 2019 study by the Pew Research Center sheds light on the gradual erosion of trust in government and other institutions.

Trust is built on the expectation that those in positions of authority will act within defined limits and in the public's best interest. When this trust is breached, whether through corruption, abuse of power, or other forms of overreach, the public's confidence in institutions and officials is significantly undermined.

According to the study, approximately 49% of Americans attribute the decline in interpersonal trust to a perception that individuals are no longer as dependable as they once were. Many connect the diminishing trust to a perceived dysfunction in the political culture, fostering suspicion and, in some cases, cynicism regarding others' capacity to discern truth from fiction.

Legitimacy is closely tied to the perception of authority acting within prescribed limits. When institutions or officials consistently overstep their authority, questions about the legitimacy of their actions and decisions arise.

The study also explored how declining trust intersects with perceptions of legitimacy, as citizens question the credibility and fairness of institutions that habitually exceed their jurisdiction and mandates.

Reputational Damage

The study conducted by Besley and Prat in 2006 delves into the intricate relationship between media, corruption, and government accountability.

While the primary focus is on the broader concept of media capture and government accountability, the findings shed light on how media coverage of corrupt practices can contribute to reputational damage.

The research underscores the pivotal role of the media in shaping public perceptions of corruption. When corrupt practices are exposed or reported widely in the media, the negative information disseminated can have profound consequences on the reputation of individuals or institutions involved. The media acts as a powerful amplifier, magnifying the impact of corrupt behavior by bringing it to the attention of a broader audience.

The findings emphasize that media coverage goes beyond merely reporting corrupt incidents; it plays a critical role in framing and disseminating information to the public. The way corruption is portrayed in the media significantly influences public opinion and perceptions. Negative information, when presented prominently and sensationally, can lead to a more damaging impact on the reputation of the individuals or entities involved.

Understanding and Respecting Authority and Jurisdiction

Understanding and respecting authority and jurisdiction is crucial for maintaining order, fostering cooperation, and promoting ethical behavior within any community or organization.

Here are some tips that can help you enhance your understanding and respect for authority and jurisdiction:

Stay Informed About Laws and Regulations

Awareness of applicable laws and regulations ensures that you are in compliance with the established legal framework. This is crucial in preventing unintentional violations that could result in legal consequences, fines, or other penalties.

Make sure you understand and adhere to laws and regulations that align with ethical conduct. It goes beyond merely avoiding legal trouble; it reflects a commitment to conducting oneself with integrity and respect for societal norms and values.

Remember, ignorance of the law is not a valid excuse. Being uninformed about the legal framework does not exempt individuals or organizations from legal consequences. Taking the time to stay informed is a proactive measure to prevent legal issues.

Consider attending training sessions or workshops that focus on legal compliance within your industry or community. These sessions often provide practical insights and interpretations of complex regulations.

If feasible, consult with legal professionals or experts who specialize in the relevant field. They can provide personalized advice and clarification on legal matters specific to your situation.

Last but not least, keep yourself updated on any changes in laws, policies, or regulations that may impact your jurisdiction. Regularly check for updates and adapt your practices accordingly to remain compliant.

Know the Chain of Command

The chain of command establishes a hierarchical structure within an organization, outlining reporting relationships and authority levels. Respecting this structure helps maintain order, clarity, and a systematic flow of information and decision-making.

Familiarize yourself with the reporting relationships within your organization. Know who your direct supervisor is and understand the hierarchy above you.

If there are changes in reporting relationships due to organizational restructuring or role changes, communicate these changes promptly to affected individuals. Transparency helps avoid confusion.

More importantly, if there are concerns or issues related to the chain of command, address them proactively. Investigate the root causes and implement corrective measures to improve adherence.

Remember, the chain of command provides a clear sense of direction and guidance. Individuals understand their reporting relationships, whom to approach for approvals, and how decisions are made. This clarity enhances overall organizational effectiveness.

Seek Permissions and Authorizations

Obtaining necessary permissions and authorizations before taking action is a fundamental aspect of respecting boundaries and avoiding overstepping within any organizational or jurisdictional context.

This process ensures that individuals or teams operate within established guidelines, minimizing the risk of conflicts and maintaining a smooth workflow.

It is important to initiate discussions with relevant stakeholders before initiating actions that may require permission. Engage in open communication to clarify expectations and seek preliminary approval.

Implement standardized request forms or documentation to formalize permission requests. Clearly articulate the proposed action, its purpose, potential impact, and the authorization sought. This ensures clarity and facilitates the approval process.

Moreover, you should always maintain a record of all authorization requests, including both approvals and denials. Documenting these decisions provides a transparent trail and helps improve future request processes.

Promote a Speak-Up Culture

Fostering a culture where employees feel empowered to speak up against abuse of authority or unethical behavior is crucial for maintaining a healthy and transparent organizational environment.

You can create multiple channels for communication within the organization. Establish regular forums, town hall meetings, or suggestion boxes where employees can express their thoughts, ideas, and concerns openly.

Clearly communicate and emphasize whistleblower protection policies. Assure employees that reporting unethical behavior or abuse of authority will not result in retaliation, and their identity will be kept confidential.

For this, implement anonymous reporting platforms, such as hotlines or online portals, where employees can submit concerns without revealing their identity. Ensure that these platforms are secure, confidential, and easily accessible.

At the same time, it is important to launch awareness campaigns specifically focused on anonymous reporting mechanisms. Use various communication channels to educate employees about the existence, purpose, and accessibility of these channels.

Put in place strict confidentiality safeguards for reported cases. Limit access to information to only those individuals involved in the investigation, protecting the anonymity of the whistleblower.

Act promptly on reported concerns. Initiate thorough investigations into reported cases of abuse of authority or unethical behavior and communicate the outcomes to employees. Prompt action reinforces trust in the reporting process.

Lead By Example

If you hold a position of authority, lead by example. Demonstrating fairness, transparency, and ethical behavior not only sets a standard for others but also contributes to earning and maintaining the respect of those within your jurisdiction.

Make decisions based on objective criteria, merit, and the best interests of the organization. Avoid favoritism and ensure that everyone is treated fairly, creating a sense of equity among team members.

Communicate openly and transparently with those under your authority. Share information relevant to their roles and the organization's goals, fostering a culture of trust and transparency.

But the most important thing is to demonstrate consistency in your actions and decisions. Consistency builds predictability and reliability, helping to establish a stable and fair working environment.

Try your best to uphold the highest ethical standards in all your interactions. Adhere to organizational values and ethical guidelines, setting a clear example for others to follow.

At the same time, don't hesitate to acknowledge and take responsibility for your mistakes. Use these instances as opportunities for learning and improvement, showing humility and accountability.

Hold yourself accountable for your actions and decisions. When leaders take responsibility, it sets the expectation that everyone in the organization should be accountable for their contributions.

Understand Professional Ethics
Familiarizing yourself with the professional ethics specific to your field or industry is a fundamental responsibility for anyone in a position of authority. Adhering to ethical standards is integral to respecting authority and maintaining integrity within a given jurisdiction.

Take the time to thoroughly understand the ethical codes and guidelines established by relevant professional associations or regulatory bodies in your industry. These codes typically outline the expected standards of behavior and conduct.

Ensure that your actions align with the ethical values and principles set by your organization. This alignment fosters a cohesive organizational culture where everyone operates within a shared ethical framework.

Adhering to professional ethics builds trust and credibility, both within your team and with external stakeholders. Consistent ethical behavior establishes a reputation for integrity and reliability.

However, it is important to prepare yourself for navigating ethical dilemmas that may arise in your role. Familiarity with professional ethics provides a foundation for making principled decisions and resolving moral challenges.

Remember to incorporate ethical considerations into your decision-making processes. Reflect on the potential ethical implications of decisions, ensuring that choices align with the broader ethical framework of your field.

In situations where ethical considerations may be complex, seek advice from ethics committees, mentors, or experts within your field. Consulting others helps in making well-informed and ethical decisions.

Act promptly to address any unethical behavior within your jurisdiction. Implement corrective measures and, if necessary, follow established disciplinary procedures. Addressing unethical behavior reinforces the importance of ethical conduct.

Seek Feedback

Foster a workplace culture that values and encourages open communication. Proactively seek feedback from team members on your leadership style, decisions, and interactions. Regularly ask for input to demonstrate that you value and appreciate diverse perspectives within the team.

But more than anything else, actively listen to the feedback you receive. Demonstrate a genuine interest in understanding the concerns raised and avoid becoming defensive. Listening attentively fosters trust and encourages more open communication.

If feedback indicates that you may be overstepping or engaging in behavior that makes others uncomfortable, address the concerns promptly.

Take time to reflect on the feedback received. Consider the validity of the concerns raised and assess whether adjustments to your behavior or decision-making processes are warranted.

If the feedback is not entirely clear or requires more context, seek clarification from those who provided the input. Understanding the specifics of their concerns enables you to make targeted and meaningful adjustments.

Communicate any adjustments or changes you plan to make based on the feedback. Transparency in addressing concerns reinforces your commitment to continuous improvement and creates a sense of accountability.

If overstepping is related to a lack of awareness or skill, consider implementing training or professional development opportunities.

A position of authority gives you power. But abusing that power or overstepping your jurisdiction can make you go toward a downward spiral, possibly leading to legal consequences and reputational damage. Remember, it can take an entire lifetime's worth of effort to build your reputation, but one wrong step can take it all away. By incorporating the tips mentioned above into your approach to authority and jurisdiction, you contribute to a positive and cooperative environment, fostering mutual respect and understanding within the framework of established rules and regulations.

Chapter 8: Overstepped Boundaries

Just like you have your personal limits, every person has a set of boundaries that they wish to maintain with others. Respecting these boundaries fosters healthy relationships and maintains a harmonious social setting for everyone.

Remember, overstepped boundaries come with dire consequences. Such actions can sow the seeds of discord, erode the foundation of trust, and strain the threads that bind individuals together.

It's essential to bear in mind that the aftermath of such transgressions can be far-reaching, impacting not only the individuals directly involved but also casting ripples across the broader social landscape.

Let's understand this concept better with the help of a story.

Boundaries Unseen: Jamie Learns a Lesson in Respect

Jamie was a high school student living in Chapel Hill, North Carolina. Despite her bright and bubbly personality and good intentions, Jamie struggled to grasp the importance of respecting the boundaries of others.

Always eager to be involved in everyone's affairs, Jamie had a tendency to pry into personal matters without considering the impact it had on her classmates.

One day, during a class project that was to be worked on in groups, Jamie's intrusive nature became particularly obvious. Ignoring the subtle signs of discomfort from group members who wished to focus on the task at hand, Jamie insisted on delving into personal issues, causing tension within the team.

As a result, what should have been a cooperative and productive project turned into an uncomfortable experience for everyone involved.

Soon, Jamie found herself all alone as her classmates started distancing themselves from her. The once lively classroom atmosphere was now tinged with unease. Jamie's well-intentioned but misguided attempts at friendship had created an environment of discomfort and strained relationships.

Coincidentally, at the same time, the school had organized a workshop on interpersonal boundaries, aiming to create awareness among students.

During the session, anecdotes were shared, and the impact of invasive behavior on personal and academic well-being was discussed openly. Although Jamie initially resisted the idea that her actions had caused harm, what she heard, particularly from her own classmates, served as a wake-up call.

And that was a turning point. Jamie was now determined to change and make amends. She started to reflect on her behavior and actively sought ways to respect the boundaries of others.

She apologized and made genuine efforts to be considerate of others. Slowly but surely, the dynamics began to shift. Classmates, appreciating Jamie's newfound awareness and efforts, began to reengage.

The school's environment shifted from one of tension to a more positive and supportive space where students felt heard and respected.

Signs of Overstepped Boundaries
In order to maintain healthy relationships and individual well-being, maintaining and respecting boundaries is paramount.

However, the subtleties of when these boundaries are crossed or violated are often complex and nuanced.

Recognizing the signs of overstepped boundaries is an essential aspect of interpersonal awareness, as it allows individuals to navigate their social landscapes with greater precision and sensitivity.

That said, let's explore the signs of overstepped boundaries by looking at some insightful research findings.

Codependency

Codependency is often characterized by an excessive reliance on others for emotional fulfillment, a disproportionate focus on meeting the needs of others to the detriment of one's own, and a lack of clear and healthy boundaries in relationships.

The book by Leonardo Tavares (2023) explores how codependency is linked to overstepped boundaries.

In codependent relationships, individuals often struggle to establish and maintain clear boundaries between themselves and others. There is a tendency to merge emotional, psychological, and even physical boundaries, leading to a lack of distinction between each person's individuality.

Codependent individuals may prioritize the needs and desires of others to an unhealthy extent, often neglecting their own well-being. This excessive focus on others can result in a continuous cycle of overstepped boundaries as personal limits are consistently compromised in the pursuit of meeting someone else's needs.

A core aspect of codependency is often a deep-seated fear of rejection or abandonment. This fear can drive individuals to go to great lengths to please others, even if it means tolerating behavior that oversteps their own boundaries.

According to Tavares, codependent individuals often struggle with assertiveness, finding it challenging to express their own needs, desires, or discomfort. This difficulty in asserting oneself can contribute to a pattern of overstepped boundaries, as the codependent individual may not communicate or enforce their limits effectively.

In such relationships, there is a high risk of enabling destructive behaviors in others. The codependent individual may tolerate or even support actions that are harmful or disrespectful, further contributing to the erosion of personal boundaries.

More importantly, the continuous neglect of one's own needs and the acceptance of overstepped boundaries can lead to profound personal dissatisfaction and a sense of unfulfillment.

Without clear boundaries, each relationship may reinforce codependent patterns, making it challenging for individuals to break free from the cycle of overstepped boundaries.

Deteriorating Relationships

The study by Parks and Floyd in 1996 explores the dynamics of online communication and delves into how interpersonal boundary violations in virtual environments can affect relationships.

The research recognizes the unique nature of online communication, where individuals engage in text-based interactions without the physical cues available in face-to-face settings. In this context, the researchers investigate how boundaries, despite the virtual nature of the environment, remain integral to the quality of relationships.

Parks and Floyd focus on individuals' perceptions of boundary violations. Whether in online or offline interactions, the study suggests that when individuals feel their personal boundaries are violated, it triggers negative emotional reactions. These violations may include unwarranted intrusions, invasions of privacy, or inappropriate behavior that transgresses the expectations of the individuals involved.

The findings highlight that when individuals perceive boundary violations, their emotional reactions can be negative. This may manifest as feelings of discomfort, frustration, or even anxiety. Emotional responses are crucial indicators of how individuals interpret and react to breaches of their personal space or expectations.

The study emphasizes the impact of perceived boundary violations on the overall quality of relationships, whether formed in cyberspace or face-to-face. When boundaries are respected, relationships tend to be more positive and satisfying. Conversely, when individuals feel their boundaries are disregarded, the quality of the relationship may deteriorate.

Parks and Floyd's research sheds light on the broader importance of respecting boundaries for maintaining positive social connections. The study underscores that the principles of boundary respect and violation extend to online environments, challenging the misconception that virtual interactions are exempt from the dynamics of interpersonal boundaries.

The study contributes to our understanding of how interpersonal dynamics, including boundary perceptions, play a crucial role in shaping the quality of relationships, even in the unique context of online communication. It highlights the need for individuals to be mindful of and respect boundaries to foster positive and satisfying social connections, whether in physical or virtual interactions.

Guilt

The study by Aurélien and Melody provides valuable insights into the role of guilt appeals in persuasion.

The findings suggest that manipulative individuals may strategically employ guilt to create emotional dependency. By making someone feel guilty for asserting their boundaries, they foster a sense of obligation and dependence, making it more likely for the person to succumb to the manipulator's desires.

Guilt can also be used to undermine an individual's confidence in their decision-making. When someone feels guilty for setting boundaries, a manipulator may exploit this emotional vulnerability to erode their confidence, making them more susceptible to influence.

Furthermore, it is possible for manipulators to use guilt to manufacture a sense of obligation in others. By framing the boundary as a source of disappointment or harm, they create a narrative that compels the individual to reconsider out of a perceived duty to avoid negative consequences.

The study emphasizes guilt as a complex emotional state that can be strategically employed in persuasive communication. Guilt appeals are designed to evoke feelings of remorse or self-blame, influencing individuals to reconsider their actions or decisions.

While guilt can be a natural emotion in relationships, using it as a manipulative tool raises ethical concerns. Healthy relationships are built on mutual respect, understanding, and the acknowledgment of individual boundaries. Manipulating others through guilt jeopardizes trust and can lead to toxic dynamics.

How to Respect Boundaries and Limits Set By Others

Respecting an individual's boundaries is a direct expression of respect for that person. The act of overstepping these limits is universally perceived as a sign of disrespect. This principle holds true across various realms of life—be it in friendships, family interactions, or professional settings.

Cultivating a mindset that values and respects boundaries becomes the cornerstone for building robust and positive connections.

While much emphasis is often placed on understanding and maintaining personal boundaries, it is equally crucial to impart the importance of respecting the limits set by others. To guide you in this aspect, here are some invaluable tips that will assist you in learning the art of respecting other people's boundaries:

Always Ask for Consent

Seeking consent is a fundamental aspect of respecting boundaries and fostering positive interpersonal relationships. It involves recognizing and valuing the autonomy of others in both physical and emotional contexts.

Besides, consistently seeking consent builds trust in relationships. It establishes a foundation of open communication and mutual understanding.

In physical interactions, asking for permission before entering someone's personal space or initiating physical contact demonstrates respect for their boundaries. Moreover, seeking consent in emotional interactions acknowledges the importance of individual feelings and psychological boundaries, contributing to emotional well-being.

When uncertain about someone's comfort level, ask clearly and directly for their consent. For example, "Is it okay if I join you?" or "Can we talk about this topic?"

In emotional conversations, ask for permission before delving into sensitive topics. For instance, "Are you comfortable discussing this right now?" Provide opt-out options when possible.

The goal is to create an environment where open communication is encouraged. Let others know they can express their comfort levels and boundaries without fear of judgment.

At the same time, it is important to educate yourself on cultural and social nuances regarding consent. Understanding different perspectives will enhance your ability to navigate diverse situations respectfully.

Be particularly mindful of power dynamics in relationships. In situations where there is a power imbalance, ensure that seeking consent is a genuine and equitable process.

Observe Nonverbal Cues

Nonverbal cues, such as facial expressions and body language, often convey emotions. Recognizing these cues helps you gauge someone's emotional state and respond appropriately.

Changes in body language and tone of voice can indicate whether someone is comfortable or uncomfortable in a particular situation. This awareness is crucial for respecting their boundaries.

Being attuned to nonverbal cues fosters empathy. It allows you to put yourself in the other person's shoes, gaining a deeper understanding of their feelings and experiences. More importantly, they complement verbal communication, providing additional context and nuance. Being mindful of these cues enhances the overall effectiveness of your communication.

For instance, sustained eye contact often indicates engagement and interest, while avoidance may suggest discomfort.

Expressions like smiles, frowns, or raised eyebrows also convey emotions. A relaxed face usually signals comfort, while tension may indicate discomfort. Observe facial expressions to gauge emotional states and adjust your approach accordingly.

Open and relaxed postures generally signify comfort, while closed or tense postures may suggest discomfort or defensiveness. Pay attention to the other person's body language, and adapt your own posture to create a comfortable environment.

Moreover, it is important to listen attentively to the tone of voice and respond with empathy to any shifts in emotion. Changes in pitch, volume, or speed can convey emotions. A calm and steady tone often indicates comfort, while variations may signal discomfort or stress.

By honing your ability to notice and interpret nonverbal cues, you become adept at understanding the unspoken aspects of communication. This heightened awareness enables you to navigate social interactions with sensitivity, respecting the comfort levels and boundaries of others in various contexts.

Respect Emotional Boundaries
Respecting emotional boundaries is fundamental to preserving trust. Pressuring someone to disclose personal issues can erode trust and make them feel vulnerable.

Remember, everyone has different comfort levels when it comes to sharing emotions. Respecting emotional boundaries contributes to the emotional well-being of individuals by allowing them to navigate their feelings at their own pace.

Providing the space for individuals to share when they are ready contributes to the creation of a safe and supportive environment. It encourages open communication based on mutual understanding.

Pressuring someone to share beyond their comfort level can create stress and discomfort. Respecting emotional boundaries helps avoid unnecessary strain on relationships.

Instead of prying with specific questions, ask open-ended ones such as "How are you feeling today?" and allow them to share as much or as little as they are comfortable with. Open-ended questions invite individuals to share voluntarily without feeling pressured.

When someone does decide to speak about their emotions, be sure to give your full attention, maintain eye contact, and avoid interrupting.

Use empathetic statements like "I'm here for you when you're ready to talk" to convey support without pressuring them. Be comfortable with moments of silence and avoid feeling the need to fill them with conversation.

More importantly, lead by example by communicating your own emotional boundaries. This encourages reciprocity in respecting personal space. Politely communicate when you're not comfortable discussing certain topics, setting a positive precedent.

Always resist the urge to push for information and allow them the time they need to share on their terms. Patience allows individuals to open up when they feel ready, promoting a more authentic sharing experience.

Accept 'No' Gracefully

Just like learning to say no is essential, accepting holds equal significance.

Accepting 'no' acknowledges and respects the autonomy of individuals. It affirms their right to make decisions about their own boundaries and preferences.

Responding to a 'no' with understanding and respect preserves the quality of relationships. It creates an atmosphere where individuals feel safe expressing their limits without fear of judgment or pressure. Plus, it builds trust by demonstrating that you value and respect the decisions of others. Trust is foundational to positive and enduring relationships.

If someone declines a request, respond with a simple and gracious acknowledgment, such as "Thank you for letting me know."

Recognize that a 'no' is not a rejection of you personally but a boundary or decision related to the specific request. It is important to reframe your perspective and understand that personal boundaries are healthy and necessary.

Pressuring someone after they've said 'no' can strain the relationship and create discomfort. So, refrain from attempting to change their mind or applying pressure. Respect their decision without further persuasion.

Resist the urge to make the person feel guilty for their decision. Acknowledge and respect their choice. Guilt-tripping can create feelings of discomfort and strain the relationship.

Be Mindful of Social Media

As social media platforms play an increasingly prominent role in our lives, it becomes crucial to be mindful of how our actions impact others.

Respecting online boundaries protects individuals' privacy. It acknowledges the right to control the information shared about oneself online.

If you want to share a photo or information about someone, ask for their consent first. Requesting permission before sharing someone else's personal information or photos shows respect for their boundaries.

Be mindful of the content you share, ensuring it aligns with your own boundaries and respects the privacy of others. Oversharing personal details or information about others can be intrusive.

Regularly review and adjust your privacy settings on social media platforms to control who can access your information.

Moreover, before tagging or mentioning someone, think about whether it aligns with their preferences and if the content is appropriate for their audience. Remember, post tags and mentions can expose them to a wider audience. Be considerate of how your actions may impact their online presence.

Some individuals may prefer limited online exposure. Respecting requests for a digital detox or reduced online presence is crucial. So, if someone requests limited tagging or mentions, respect their decision and refrain from including them in extensive online activities.

Apologize and Learn

In any relationship, whether personal or professional, it's inevitable that boundaries may be unintentionally crossed from time to time. When such instances occur, offering a sincere apology is a vital step toward repairing any potential harm and demonstrating a commitment to respecting the other person's limits.

Always remember apologizing sincerely is a key element in rebuilding trust. It communicates that you recognize the importance of the other person's boundaries and are committed to learning from the experience.

Begin your apology by expressing regret for any discomfort or harm caused by your actions. Acknowledge that you are taking responsibility for the overstepped boundary, demonstrating accountability for your actions.

Clearly articulate what boundary was crossed to ensure mutual understanding and to address the specific issue.

If the other person seeks an explanation, provide one without justifying or excusing your behavior. This helps in understanding but does not diminish the apology.

Express empathy for the other person's feelings and reassure them that you understand the impact of your actions. At the same time, it is important to demonstrate a genuine commitment to learning from the experience and avoiding similar mistakes in the future.

If appropriate, ask the other person for guidance on how to better respect their boundaries in the future. More importantly, you should respect the other person's need for space and time to process the apology and the situation.

Reflect on the incident, learn from it, and take proactive steps to educate yourself on respecting boundaries.

Create Mutual Agreements

Establishing mutual agreements ensures that both parties have a shared understanding of each other's expectations, preferences, and boundaries. This clarity is fundamental to a healthy and harmonious relationship.

Mutual agreements are crafted through consideration of each individual's needs and comfort levels. This process fosters a sense of respect for the uniqueness of each person in the relationship.

Begin by expressing your willingness to discuss and establish mutual agreements in the relationship. Take turns expressing your needs and boundaries, and actively listen to your partner's input.

Clearly define the boundaries that are important to each person. This clarity reduces the likelihood of unintentional boundary crossings. Discuss and agree upon specific boundaries related to personal space, communication preferences, and any other aspects relevant to the relationship.

Acknowledge that mutual agreements may require compromise. Flexibility ensures that the relationship dynamic remains balanced and considerate of both parties.

More than anything else, understand the fact that relationships evolve, and so do individual needs. Regularly review and adjust mutual agreements to reflect changes in circumstances or personal growth.

By incorporating the strategies mentioned above into your interactions, you contribute to a culture of mutual respect, understanding, and healthy communication. Respecting boundaries is an ongoing process that requires continuous effort and a commitment to creating positive and supportive relationships.

Chapter 9: Negotiating Ethical Crossroads in Life

Ethical boundaries define the morally acceptable limits of behavior within a given context or relationship. These boundaries serve as guidelines that help individuals navigate interactions and decisions while upholding principles of honesty, integrity, and respect for others.

Ethical boundaries vary across cultures, professions, and personal beliefs, but they generally involve considerations such as truthfulness, confidentiality, and the avoidance of harm.

Adhering to ethical boundaries promotes trust, fairness, and a sense of responsibility in both personal and professional settings. Straying beyond these boundaries can lead to ethical dilemmas, compromised relationships, and potential harm to individuals or communities.

In life, every person comes across ethical crossroads at least once or twice. But how you navigate these dilemmas defines you as a person. Let's understand this concept better with the help of a story.

Bound By Integrity: Ted's Decision

Ted was a hard-working man living in New York. One day, he found himself facing a deep ethical dilemma.

Ted's sister, Emily, desperate to secure a job for her struggling son, Michael, approached Ted with a request that tested the boundaries of fairness and meritocracy. Emily pleaded with Ted to use his influence as a senior manager in a reputable company to secure a position for Michael, even though he lacked the necessary qualifications.

Caught between family loyalty and his commitment to ethical principles, Ted struggled to make a decision. The city's competitive job market and the pressures faced by his nephew made Emily's plea even more compelling. However, Ted understood the importance of maintaining integrity in professional matters.

After careful consideration, Ted chose to uphold his ethical boundaries. He believed that compromising the merit-based hiring process not only jeopardized the reputation of the company but also undermined the principles of fairness and equal opportunity. In a long and honest conversation with Emily, Ted explained his decision, expressing empathy for Michael's situation but emphasizing the importance of fairness in professional settings.

Instead of using his position to secure an undeserved opportunity, Ted offered to mentor Michael, providing guidance and support to help him develop the necessary skills and qualifications for a competitive job market.

While the initial conversation was challenging, Ted's commitment to ethical conduct ultimately strengthened his relationship with both his sister and nephew, demonstrating that one could navigate difficult situations with integrity and compassion.

Eventually, thanks to Ted's efforts in mentoring him, Micheal was able to land a job at another reputable firm.

Significance of Ethical Boundaries

Ethical boundaries serve as the guiding principles that delineate the acceptable limits of behavior within personal, professional, and societal contexts. Rooted in fundamental principles of integrity, fairness, and responsibility, these boundaries play a crucial role in shaping the character of individuals and organizations.

The significance of ethical boundaries extends beyond mere compliance with rules and regulations; it encompasses the cultivation of trust, the preservation of reputation, and the promotion of positive social contributions.

As society navigates complex challenges and dynamic environments, understanding and upholding ethical boundaries become paramount for fostering relationships built on trust, sustaining organizational excellence, and contributing to the broader well-being of communities.

Let's understand the importance of staying within ethical limits by looking at some insightful research findings.

Trust and Reputation
The study conducted by Mayer et al. in 1995 delves into the intricate relationship between trust and ethical behavior within interpersonal relationships. The research underscores the pivotal role that trust plays in shaping the dynamics of relationships and organizations, emphasizing the profound influence of ethical conduct on the establishment and maintenance of trust.

Mayer and his co-authors propose an integrative model that explores the multifaceted nature of organizational trust. The model posits that trust is built upon the perception of the trustee's ability, benevolence, and integrity.

Importantly, the dimension of integrity aligns closely with ethical behavior. The study contends that individuals are more likely to trust those who are perceived as having high moral and ethical standards.

Ethical behavior, according to the model, contributes significantly to the perceived integrity of individuals or organizations. When individuals consistently demonstrate ethical conduct, they are viewed as reliable, principled, and trustworthy. This, in turn, fosters a positive environment for the development and sustenance of interpersonal relationships within an organizational context.

The findings of Mayer et al.'s study affirm the intrinsic connection between ethical behavior and trust, highlighting that individuals who prioritize ethical principles are more likely to be perceived as trustworthy. This correlation between ethics and trust has profound implications for personal relationships, team dynamics, and organizational success.

As individuals and organizations uphold ethical boundaries, they not only contribute to the cultivation of trust but also enhance their reputation as reliable and principled entities in the eyes of others.

Individual Well-Being

Tangney's 2000 research sheds light on the intricate relationship between ethical behavior and psychological well-being, particularly emphasizing the emotional consequences for individuals who engage in unethical conduct. The study explores the psychological impact of unethical behavior, highlighting the prevalence of guilt and anxiety as significant indicators of compromised mental health.

Ethical behavior, defined by adherence to moral principles and societal norms, contributes to a sense of personal integrity and alignment with one's values. Tangney's findings suggest that individuals who prioritize ethical conduct are more likely to experience positive psychological well-being. This positive well-being may manifest in the form of enhanced self-esteem, greater life satisfaction, and improved overall mental health.

Conversely, the study underscores the adverse effects associated with engaging in unethical behavior. Tangney suggests that individuals who deviate from ethical standards, whether through dishonesty, betrayal, or other unethical actions, often grapple with intense emotions such as guilt and anxiety. Guilt, in this context, emerges as a powerful emotional response triggered by a perceived violation of one's own moral code or societal norms.

Guilt, as a consequence of unethical behavior, can lead to persistent feelings of remorse and self-condemnation. This emotional burden, in turn, can contribute to heightened anxiety, further impacting an individual's mental health.

The internal conflict arising from a breach of ethical boundaries can create a cycle of negative emotions, potentially leading to stress, diminished self-esteem, and a compromised sense of well-being.

Social Responsibility

Carroll's research in 1999, particularly his work on corporate social responsibility (CSR), emphasizes the significant relationship between ethical behavior and contributions to societal well-being. The study delves into the idea that individuals and organizations who prioritize ethical practices are more inclined to engage in activities that benefit society, extending beyond mere compliance with legal requirements.

The concept of social responsibility encompasses the ethical obligation of individuals and organizations to consider the broader impact of their actions on society. Carroll's research suggests that ethical behavior is a foundational element of social responsibility.

When individuals and organizations adhere to ethical principles, they are more likely to align their activities with the values and expectations of the communities they serve.

One key aspect of this alignment is reflected in the positive contributions that ethical actors make to society. These contributions can take various forms, such as philanthropy, environmental stewardship, fair employment practices, and community engagement.

Ethical behavior involves not only avoiding harm but actively seeking opportunities to enhance the well-being of the communities in which individuals and organizations operate.

Moreover, the research suggests that there is a reciprocal relationship between ethical behavior and social responsibility. Engaging in socially responsible activities can, in turn, reinforce an ethical reputation. This positive feedback loop creates a culture where ethical behavior becomes intertwined with a commitment to societal improvement.

In a broader context, the findings of Carroll's research emphasize that ethical behavior is a cornerstone of responsible citizenship, whether at an individual or organizational level.

By considering the impact of decisions and actions on society, ethical actors contribute to the creation of a more sustainable, just, and equitable world. Thus, ethical behavior not only fulfills a moral obligation but also becomes a driving force behind positive social change, reflecting a comprehensive understanding of social responsibility in its truest sense.

Navigating Ethical Dilemmas with Integrity

In almost all personal and professional endeavors, ethical dilemmas are inevitable.

Navigating these moral crossroads requires a steadfast commitment to integrity—a compass that guides one's actions with unwavering honesty and principled conduct.

That said, here are some useful tips and tricks that will help you maintain integrity when facing ethical challenges:

Define Your Values

Defining personal and professional values is a foundational step for ethical decision-making. Start by listing the values that are most important to you personally and professionally. These could include honesty, integrity, responsibility, empathy, teamwork, innovation, or any other principles that resonate with you.

Prioritize your values based on their significance in different aspects of your life. Consider which values are non-negotiable and should guide your decisions in all circumstances.

Be sure to reflect on past experiences where your values were tested or where you felt a strong sense of alignment with your values. Identify what worked well and what values were particularly important in those situations.

More importantly, develop a personal code of ethics that concisely captures your core values and principles. This could be a written document or a mental checklist that you can refer to when faced with ethical decisions.

Use your values as criteria when faced with decisions. Before making a choice, evaluate how each option aligns with your core principles. This structured approach can guide you in choosing the most ethical course of action.

But don't forget to review and update your values periodically. As you grow personally and professionally, your priorities may shift. Regularly revisiting and adjusting your values ensures that they remain relevant and meaningful.

Consider Consequences

Evaluating the potential consequences of your choices requires a thoughtful consideration of the impact on oneself, others directly involved, and the broader community.

Start by considering how each option may affect you personally in the short term. Evaluate the potential consequences on your well-being, reputation, and immediate circumstances. This involves reflecting on whether a decision aligns with your values and whether it might lead to personal discomfort or conflict.

Next, assess how each option may impact individuals directly involved in the situation. Consider their perspectives, emotions, and potential reactions. This involves anticipating how your decision may affect relationships, trust, and collaboration in the immediate aftermath.

Extend your analysis to the broader community or stakeholders who may be affected by your decision. Consider the immediate implications for the community, such as any potential harm, disruption, or positive outcomes. This could involve thinking about how the decision aligns with community expectations and values.

At the same time, don't forget to project how each option may affect you in the long term. Consider the potential consequences for your personal and professional growth, reputation, and relationships over an extended period. This involves thinking about the sustainability and alignment of your decision with your long-term goals.

Anticipate the long-term consequences for individuals directly impacted by your decision. Consider how relationships may evolve, trust may be built or eroded, and the overall well-being of others may be affected. This involves thinking beyond immediate reactions to potential lasting effects.

Be mindful of unintended consequences that may arise from your decision. Consider how unforeseen outcomes could affect both yourself and others. This involves thinking critically about potential ripple effects that may not be immediately apparent.

Seek Different Perspectives

Seeking diverse perspectives from trusted colleagues, mentors, or friends is a valuable strategy in navigating ethical dilemmas, as it brings multiple viewpoints to the decision-making process.

Begin by identifying individuals whom you trust and respect for their judgment.

Foster an open and confidential environment for discussion. Assure your advisors that their input is valued and that you seek their perspectives to make a well-informed and ethical decision.

Clearly articulate the ethical dilemma, providing context, relevant details, and the options you are considering. Clarity in communication ensures that your advisors have a comprehensive understanding of the situation.

Encourage your advisors to provide honest and candid feedback. Emphasize that you are open to hearing different viewpoints, even if they challenge your initial thoughts. This openness fosters a more fruitful discussion.

Seek advisors with diverse expertise and backgrounds. Having individuals with different professional experiences, cultural perspectives, or areas of expertise can bring a well-rounded understanding of the ethical dilemma.

Consider the Golden Rule

Applying the Golden Rule—treat others as you would like to be treated—adds a crucial empathetic dimension to ethical decision-making.

Take a moment to empathize with the individuals directly affected by your decision. Imagine yourself in their position, experiencing the consequences of each potential choice. Consider how you would feel, what concerns you might have, and what expectations you would hold.

Reflect on the emotional impact your decision might have on others. If the decision involves potentially negative consequences, consider the emotional toll it may take.

Assess the fairness of your decision from the perspective of those affected. Consider whether the decision treats everyone equitably and upholds principles of justice. This ensures that your actions are guided by a sense of fairness and equality.

Anticipate how others might react to your decision. Envision the potential responses and consider whether you would find those responses reasonable and fair if you were in their position.

If appropriate, communicate openly about your decision. Provide transparent explanations and address concerns. This openness reflects the kind of communication you would appreciate if roles were reversed.

Last but not least, be open to learning from the experience. If your decision has unintended consequences or is not well-received, reflect on what adjustments you could make in the future. A learning-oriented approach will reflect your commitment to continuous improvement and ethical growth.

Take Your Time

Ethical dilemmas often evoke strong emotions. Taking a step back allows individuals to gain emotional distance from the situation. This emotional space is essential for making decisions with a clear and rational mindset, free from the immediate influence of intense feelings.

Reflection provides an opportunity to consider multiple perspectives. By stepping back, individuals can engage in a more comprehensive analysis, taking into account various viewpoints and potential consequences.

Always remember hasty decisions in the face of ethical dilemmas can lead to unintended consequences. Only make a final decision after careful consideration of all aspects.

Taking some time for evaluation will also make you feel confident in your choice.

Be Prepared to Take Responsibility

No matter how careful you may be, mistakes are bound to happen.

If you recognize that a mistake has been made, acknowledge it promptly. Avoid delays in taking responsibility, as timely acknowledgment demonstrates accountability and a commitment to ethical behavior.

Clearly communicate your acknowledgment of the mistake. Be transparent about what went wrong, why it happened, and the steps you plan to take to rectify the situation. Open communication builds trust.

Offer a sincere and genuine apology to those affected by the mistake. Acknowledge any harm caused and express your commitment to making amends.

Develop a concrete plan to rectify the mistake. This may involve revisiting the decision, implementing corrective measures, or collaborating with others to find solutions. Clearly outline the steps you intend to take.

If appropriate, involve stakeholders in the process of rectification. Seek their input and collaboration in finding solutions.

More importantly, use the mistake as an opportunity to learn and improve. Implement changes in processes, decision-making frameworks, or communication strategies to prevent similar mistakes in the future.

Consider the "Front-Page Test"

The "Front-Page Test" is a valuable tool in ethical decision-making that encourages individuals to assess the public perception and potential scrutiny of their decisions.

Imagine that your decision, along with the details surrounding it, will be exposed to the public eye on the front page of a newspaper. Consider whether you are comfortable with the level of transparency the decision would receive.

Assess how well you can justify and explain your decision to the public. Consider whether the rationale behind your choice aligns with ethical principles, organizational values, and societal expectations.

Reflect on the ethical implications of your decision. Evaluate whether the decision upholds moral standards, legal requirements, and societal norms. If your decision aligns with these ethical considerations, it is more likely to withstand public scrutiny.

Strive to evaluate your decision objectively, as if you were an impartial observer. Think of whether an unbiased observer would view your decision as ethical, fair, and in the best interest of all relevant parties.

Don't forget to assess whether your decision complies with legal and regulatory requirements. If your actions are in accordance with the law, it contributes to the defensibility and integrity of your decision.

By approaching ethical dilemmas with a commitment to your values, consideration of consequences, and a willingness to seek guidance, you can navigate these challenges with integrity, fostering trust and maintaining a strong ethical foundation in your personal and professional life.

Chapter 10: Balancing Work and Life

Setting boundaries is like drawing lines on a map of life – not just for ethics and laws, but for juggling work and personal stuff. When those lines get fuzzy, it's like losing the beat of a great song with two important tunes.

Think about it: just like rules keep our society ticking, boundaries between work and life are like little life rules. When you let those rules slide, it's like a messy mashup of job stress creeping into almost everything, be it your me-time or family matters.

Respecting the line between your job and your life isn't just about getting stuff done efficiently. It's about giving each part of your life the attention it deserves. Keeping those lines intact lets you be all in – be it thriving in your career or savoring happy moments.

If you let work take over your personal space, you might miss out on the simple joys of life. But if your personal matters start to hog the work spotlight, it could mess up your career groove.

To live a happy and balanced life, you have to set your limits, make them clear, and stick to them.

That said, let's understand the significance of boundaries in maintaining work-life balance with the help of a story.

Balancing Act: Sarah's Journey

Sarah was a talented graphic designer working in Austin, Texas. Sarah was known for her creativity and professionalism. However, at one point, the boundaries between her work and personal life started to blur.

Sarah struggled to wrap her head around the complexities of her recent divorce. The emotional toll of the separation, coupled with the challenges of co-parenting, began to cast a shadow over her once-thriving professional life.

As deadlines loomed and client demands escalated, Sarah found it increasingly difficult to compartmentalize her personal matters.

One day, a crucial design project for a high-profile client was on the line. The creative spark that usually fueled Sarah's artistic endeavors was dimmed by the turmoil in her personal life. Juggling custody arrangements and navigating emotional conversations during work hours became the norm, eroding the boundaries that once separated her personal and professional worlds.

The impact was deep. Missed deadlines, overlooked details, and a general sense of distraction permeated Sarah's work. Ultimately, Sarah reached a breaking point. It became clear that the emotional turbulence of her personal life was infiltrating the sanctuary of her professional space. The creative energy that once flowed freely now felt stifled.

In a moment of introspection, Sarah decided to take a step back. Seeking support from friends, she started attending therapy to navigate the emotional complexities of her divorce.

Slowly, she began to establish healthier boundaries, carving out dedicated work hours and designating personal time for self-care.

The journey towards regaining work-life balance was slow but fruitful. As Sarah's emotional well-being improved, so did her professional focus. With newfound clarity, she was able to channel her creative spirit into her designs once again.

Importance of Maintaining a Healthy Work-Life Balance

In the ever-evolving landscape of modern work, the struggle to achieve a healthy work-life balance stands as a paramount challenge. Yet, when it comes to navigating professional responsibilities and personal aspirations, the establishment and maintenance of clear boundaries remain the one true solution for overall well-being and success.

Let's understand the significance of maintaining boundaries for a harmonious work-life balance by looking at some insightful research findings.

Reduced Stress and Burnout

Kossek and Thompson's 2012 research provides valuable insights into the relationship between boundary-setting and stress levels, as well as the prevalence of burnout among individuals. The study contributes significantly to our understanding of the impact that clear work-life boundaries can have on overall well-being.

The research suggests that individuals who consciously establish and maintain clear boundaries between their work and personal lives experience lower levels of stress. This finding aligns with the notion that when individuals can compartmentalize and separate their professional responsibilities from their personal lives, they are better equipped to manage the demands of each domain without undue interference from the other.

The concept of work-life boundaries, as explored in Kossek and Thompson's research, goes beyond the physical separation of time and space. It also encompasses the psychological and emotional aspects of creating a distinct divide between work-related stressors and personal life. When individuals are successful in outlining these boundaries, they are less likely to carry the stressors from work into their personal time.

Moreover, the study sheds light on the crucial link between well-established boundaries and reduced burnout. Burnout, characterized by emotional exhaustion, depersonalization, and a diminished sense of personal accomplishment, is a pervasive issue in today's professional landscape. The research's findings suggest that individuals who are proactive in setting boundaries are more resilient to the factors that contribute to burnout.

The research highlights the proactive role individuals can play in boundary management. It's not merely about the external constraints imposed by organizational policies but about the intentional efforts individuals make to create a clear separation between their work and personal lives.

In practical terms, this might involve setting specific work hours, designating dedicated personal time, and refraining from engaging in work-related tasks during non-working hours. By doing so, individuals can create a protective buffer that shields them from the potentially deleterious effects of work-related stress and burnout.

Positive Impact on Mental Health

The research conducted by Nominan et al., 2023 contributes significantly to our understanding of the intricate interplay between work-life balance, mental health, and overall life satisfaction. The findings of this study underscore the positive association between maintaining a balance between work and personal life and various facets of individual well-being.

The research indicates that individuals who successfully strike a balance between their professional and personal spheres tend to experience improved mental health. This connection implies that the ability to allocate time and energy effectively to both work and personal life contributes to reduced stress, anxiety, and other mental health challenges.

The study suggests that by avoiding the extremes of overcommitment to work or neglecting personal life, individuals can create a more conducive environment for positive mental well-being.

Furthermore, the research emphasizes that this balance is not only instrumental in preventing negative mental health outcomes but also in enhancing overall life satisfaction. Individuals who manage to harmonize the demands of their work with their personal aspirations report a higher level of contentment and fulfillment in their lives. This positive correlation suggests that the benefits of a well-managed work-life balance extend beyond the professional realm, influencing the broader spectrum of one's overall life experience.

In practical terms, the study implies that strategies such as setting clear boundaries, prioritizing self-care, and being mindful of time management can contribute to achieving a balance between work and personal life. By recognizing the importance of both domains and actively working to integrate them harmoniously, individuals are more likely to experience positive outcomes in terms of mental health and life satisfaction.

The implications of this research extend beyond individual well-being and have relevance for organizations and policymakers aiming to foster healthier work environments. It suggests that promoting practices and policies that support work-life balance not only benefits employees' mental health but also contributes to a more satisfied and engaged workforce.

Enhanced Family and Social Relationships
The research conducted by Kreiner et al., 2009 delves into the intricate dynamics of the work-home interface and the impact

of boundary work tactics on individuals' ability to allocate time and energy to family and social relationships. The findings of this study shed light on the crucial role that clear boundaries play in nurturing and strengthening connections beyond the professional world.

The research suggests that individuals who are adept at establishing clear boundaries between their work and personal lives are better positioned to allocate dedicated time and energy to their family and social relationships. This intentional separation allows individuals to compartmentalize their professional responsibilities, creating distinct spaces for personal connections to thrive.

By delineating these boundaries, individuals can protect and prioritize the moments spent with family members and friends. The study implies that when work-related demands encroach upon personal time, it can jeopardize the quality and depth of familial and social interactions. Conversely, when individuals proactively set boundaries, they create a framework that facilitates a more meaningful engagement with their loved ones.

The concept of "boundary work tactics," as explored in this research, refers to the strategies individuals employ to manage the interface between their work and personal life effectively. This could involve setting specific time slots for family activities, establishing rules for not engaging in work-related tasks during personal time, or adopting mindfulness practices to transition between work and home roles.

The positive impact of these boundary work tactics on family and social relationships is significant. The study suggests that fostering stronger connections in these domains contributes not only to the individual's personal well-being but also to the resilience and cohesion of the family unit and social circles.

In practical terms, the research encourages individuals to be proactive in defining and defending their personal time. It emphasizes the importance of effective communication and negotiation of boundaries both within the workplace and at home. By doing so, individuals can create a conducive environment for the cultivation and maintenance of meaningful connections outside of the professional context.

How to Create Work-Life Balance

While both personal and professional lives hold equal importance, it is imperative that you learn to strike a balance between the two. When the balance gets disrupted, it can directly impact your well-being.

The best approach to creating an equilibrium is to set boundaries. That said, here are some tips that will help you create a harmonious work-life balance:

Establish Work and Personal Boundaries

Establishing clear boundaries between work and personal life is vital for maintaining a healthy balance. Consider developing a structured daily or weekly schedule that outlines when you'll be focusing on work tasks and when you'll engage in personal activities. Stick to this schedule as closely as possible.

At the same time, it is essential to communicate your boundaries to colleagues, clients, and even friends or family members. Let them know when you'll be available for work-related matters and when you'll be focusing on personal commitments.

Understand your limits and be willing to say no when additional work tasks or commitments threaten to invade your personal time. Setting boundaries also involves knowing when to decline additional responsibilities.

Schedule self-care activities during your personal time and treat them with the same level of importance as work tasks. Whether it's exercise, hobbies, or relaxation, these activities contribute to a balanced and fulfilling life.

More importantly, regularly assess the effectiveness of your boundaries. If certain strategies are not working, be open to adjusting and refining your approach to better suit your evolving needs and circumstances.

Create a Realistic Schedule

A realistic schedule that accommodates both work and personal commitments is essential for maintaining a healthy work-life balance.

Evaluate the time you have available each day and week. Consider your work hours, commute time, and other non-negotiable commitments. Identify and prioritize both work-related tasks and personal commitments. Recognize the most critical and time-sensitive responsibilities in each category.

Assign specific time blocks for work tasks and personal activities. Clearly define when you'll be engaged in work and when you'll dedicate time to personal matters.

Be mindful of including breaks and downtime in your schedule. These moments are crucial for recharging and avoiding burnout. Allocate short breaks during work hours and plan periods of relaxation during personal time.

More importantly, resist the temptation to overcommit yourself. Ensure that your schedule allows for flexibility and unexpected developments. Overloading your agenda can lead to stress and hinder your ability to meet commitments effectively.

Understand that it's not possible to do everything at once. Learn to prioritize tasks and commitments based on their importance and deadlines. This helps you focus on what truly matters in both your professional and personal life.

Establish realistic goals for your work and personal life. Avoid setting unrealistic expectations that may lead to frustration and disappointment. Setting achievable goals contributes to a sense of accomplishment.

Don't forget to incorporate buffer time in your schedule to account for unexpected delays or additional time needed for tasks. Having a cushion ensures that you're not constantly rushing from one commitment to the next.

Create a Dedicated Workspace

Establishing a designated workspace at home, especially if you work remotely, is an important part of separating work and personal life.

You see, designating a specific area for work creates a physical separation between your professional and personal life. This boundary helps signal when you are in "work mode" and when you are in "personal mode."

Besides, having a dedicated workspace has a profound psychological impact. It helps condition your mind to associate that particular area with work-related tasks, enhancing focus and productivity during designated work hours.

Identify a specific area in your home that will serve as your workspace. Ideally, this should be a quiet, well-lit, and comfortable space.

Invest in ergonomic furniture, such as a comfortable chair and a suitable desk. Ensure that the setup promotes good posture and minimizes discomfort during long work hours.

Consider using physical boundaries or visual cues to demarcate your workspace. This could be achieved through the arrangement of furniture or the addition of plants or decorative elements.

Clearly define your work hours and communicate them to those sharing your living space. Stick to these hours as closely as possible to maintain a structured routine.

Establish clear rules for yourself when you're in your workspace. This might include no personal calls, limited social media use, or any other guidelines that help maintain focus.

Designate specific areas for breaks within your home. This separation reinforces the idea that breaks occur outside of your workspace, contributing to a healthier work-life balance.

Delegate and Outsource
Delegating tasks, whether at work or at home, is a strategic approach that not only lightens your workload but also allows you to optimize your time and energy for tasks that truly require your attention.

Start by identifying tasks that do not necessarily require your unique skills or expertise. These could be routine, time-consuming, or tasks that others in your team or household can handle competently.

Recognize your strengths and limitations. Delegate tasks that align with others' strengths, enabling a more efficient and effective completion of those responsibilities.

Remember, outsourcing and delegation are opportunities for skill development. Empower individuals by giving them the autonomy to make decisions and take ownership of the tasks assigned to them. This not only benefits you but also contributes to their professional or personal growth.

Recognize when outsourcing certain responsibilities is more efficient than managing them internally. Whether it's hiring a professional service or seeking external support, outsourcing can be a strategic move to save time and resources.

Take Vacation Time

Vacation time provides a crucial opportunity to step away from the daily stresses of work. It allows your mind and body to relax, reducing the levels of stress hormones and promoting a sense of calm. So, don't hesitate to make the most of your paid time off.

Communicate your vacation plans to colleagues and set clear boundaries regarding your availability during this time. Use email auto-replies and communicate your unavailability in advance to manage expectations.

Actively disconnect from work-related emails, messages, and tasks during your vacation. Create a digital detox plan to ensure you are not constantly tethered to work obligations.

Plan leisure activities that bring you joy and relaxation. Whether it's a beach vacation, a nature retreat, or exploring a new city, choose activities that align with your interests and help you unwind.

But the most important part is to make quality sleep a priority during your vacation. Allow yourself to catch up on any sleep deficit and establish a healthy sleep routine that contributes to your overall well-being.

Spend quality time with family and friends. Strengthening personal relationships contributes significantly to your emotional well-being and adds a positive dimension to your vacation experience.

If longer vacations are challenging, plan shorter getaways or extended weekends. Even a brief change of scenery can have a meaningful impact on your well-being.

Communicate Openly

If personal issues are affecting your work, consider having an open and honest conversation with your supervisor or HR department.

Select an appropriate time and setting for the conversation. Ideally, schedule a private meeting where you can discuss your concerns without interruptions.

Before the meeting, organize your thoughts and be clear about the personal issues affecting your work. Outline how these issues are impacting your performance and well-being.

While discussing personal challenges, shift the focus toward potential solutions. Consider proposing ways in which your workload can be managed, suggest reasonable accommodations, or discuss a temporary adjustment to your responsibilities.

You can also seek guidance on how the company can support you during challenging times. This might involve adjustments to your workload, flexible working arrangements, or access to employee assistance programs.

If personal issues are significantly impacting your well-being, consider seeking professional help, such as counseling or therapy. A trained professional can provide guidance and support during challenging times.

Remember that work-life balance is a dynamic and personal concept. What works for one person may not work for another, so it's essential to tailor the tips mentioned above to fit your unique circumstances and preferences.

Chapter 11: Thriving Within Limits: The Role of Self-Reflection

Self-reflection serves as a powerful tool for comprehending one's limits and flourishing within them. Taking a moment to introspect allows individuals to identify their strengths and weaknesses, enabling a realistic understanding of their capabilities.

By acknowledging personal limitations, one can make informed decisions, set achievable goals, and optimize their efforts. This self-awareness acts as a compass, guiding individuals towards activities and pursuits that align with their skills and passions.

Embracing boundaries doesn't signify defeat; instead, it fosters a sense of self-compassion and resilience. Through self-reflection, people gain insights that empower them to navigate challenges wisely, capitalize on strengths, and cultivate a fulfilling life within the parameters of their unique abilities.

Let's understand the role of self-reflection in understanding limits with the help of a story.

Adapt and Inspire: Marcus's Journey

Marcus was an ambitious high school science teacher in Chicago, Michigan. Marcus dreamed of revolutionizing the way students perceived science. He aimed to make his classes exciting, dynamic, and unforgettable. However, his initial attempts to incorporate cutting-edge experiments and unconventional teaching methods didn't yield the expected results, leaving him frustrated and questioning his approach.

After a particularly challenging semester, Marcus decided to take a break from the classroom chaos and found himself taking a stroll in the local park.

As the city skyline glittered in the background, he reflected on his journey and realized that, in his zeal to inspire, he had neglected to recognize the diverse learning styles and challenges of his students.

Empowered by this revelation, Marcus embarked on a mission of self-improvement. He attended workshops on innovative teaching techniques, collaborated with fellow educators, and sought feedback from his students.

Through introspection, he discovered that embracing adaptability and understanding the individual needs of his students was the key to success.

Back in the classroom, Marcus implemented a tailored approach to teaching. He introduced interactive experiments, incorporated real-world applications of scientific concepts, and provided additional support to students who needed it. The transformation was remarkable. Students became engaged, curiosity flourished, and test scores soared.

Outside the classroom, Marcus fostered a sense of community among his students by organizing science fairs and field trips to Chicago's renowned museums and laboratories. He realized that education extended beyond textbooks and classrooms, and the city became an extension of his teaching toolkit.

How Self-Reflection Leads to Personal Growth

Personal growth is an ongoing process, but self-reflection becomes the fuel that propagates your development.

The art of self-reflection is not merely a contemplative exercise; rather, it serves as a dynamic process that illuminates the contours of your thoughts, emotions, and behaviors.

Let's explore how introspection can help with personal development by looking at some insightful research findings.

Clarification of Values and Goals

The research conducted by Sheldon and Kasser in 2001 highlights a pivotal aspect of self-reflection – its role in clarifying personal values and aligning actions with those values. This process, when effectively undertaken, contributes significantly to fostering a sense of purpose and direction in life.

Self-reflection provides individuals with a designated space for introspection, enabling them to identify and articulate their core values. These values represent the fundamental principles and beliefs that guide one's decisions, behaviors, and priorities in life. Understanding these values lays the foundation for creating a framework through which individuals can navigate their journey.

The research suggests that the true impact of self-reflection is realized when individuals consciously align their actions with their identified values. This alignment involves making intentional choices and decisions that resonate with one's core beliefs. When actions are congruent with personal values, individuals experience a profound sense of authenticity and integrity in their endeavors.

The alignment of actions with personal values is closely tied to a sense of purpose in life. As individuals engage in activities and pursue goals that reflect their deeply held values, they cultivate a purposeful existence. This sense of purpose serves as a motivational force, providing meaning and direction to daily endeavors.

When faced with choices and dilemmas, individuals who have engaged in self-reflection and established clarity regarding their values possess a valuable decision-making tool.

The research implies that the process of aligning actions with personal values is intricately linked to overall well-being.

Individuals who live authentically, guided by their values, often report higher levels of life satisfaction, happiness, and a sense of fulfillment.

The long-term satisfaction derived from living in alignment with one's values goes beyond momentary happiness. It reflects a sustained and meaningful approach to life, where each decision and action contributes to a cohesive narrative that aligns with one's fundamental beliefs.

Improved Problem-Solving Skills

The study conducted by Grant, Franklin, and Langford in 2002 sheds light on a valuable aspect of self-reflection – its association with improved problem-solving skills. This research suggests that engaging in regular self-reflection, particularly through the critical evaluation of past experiences and decisions, empowers individuals to identify patterns and cultivate more effective strategies for overcoming challenges.

Regular self-reflection involves looking back at past experiences and decisions with a discerning eye. This retrospective analysis allows individuals to gain insights into the outcomes of their actions, understand the factors influencing those outcomes, and identify patterns that may emerge across various situations.

Furthermore, self-reflection encourages individuals to acknowledge and learn from their mistakes. Instead of viewing failures as setbacks, the focus shifts toward extracting valuable lessons from them. This learning-oriented approach contributes to an adaptive mindset that is open to growth and improvement.

Armed with insights gained from self-reflection, individuals can strategically adjust their approaches to problem-solving. This might involve modifying decision-making processes, adopting alternative strategies, or honing specific skills that are identified as crucial in overcoming challenges.

Individuals become more flexible in their thinking and problem-solving as they draw on a wealth of accumulated knowledge and insights gained through self-reflection.

Engaging in regular self-reflection also establishes a continuous improvement cycle. As individuals implement new strategies, observe outcomes, and reflect on the effectiveness of those strategies, they perpetuate a dynamic process of growth and refinement in their problem-solving abilities.

The benefits of improved problem-solving skills through self-reflection are transferable across various life domains – from personal relationships and professional endeavors to academic pursuits. The skills honed through this process contribute to a holistic approach to navigating life's challenges.

Mindfulness-Based Interventions

Mindfulness-based interventions, rooted in the pioneering work of Jon Kabat-Zinn and others, have gained recognition for their transformative impact on individuals' self-awareness and understanding of personal limits.

These practices, often derived from mindfulness meditation, guide individuals to cultivate a heightened awareness of their thoughts, emotions, and physical sensations in the present moment. The process involves observing these experiences without judgment, creating a space for a more nuanced understanding of personal boundaries.

Mindfulness emphasizes anchoring attention in the present moment. By cultivating awareness of the here and now, individuals engage in a continuous observation of their thoughts and feelings as they unfold. This heightened present-moment awareness allows for a real-time understanding of one's mental and emotional landscape.

Central to mindfulness is the practice of non-judgmental observation. Instead of labeling thoughts or emotions as 'good' or 'bad,' individuals learn to observe them objectively. This absence of judgment creates a non-reactive space, enabling a clearer perception of personal experiences and, consequently, personal limits.

Furthermore, mindfulness is also associated with improved emotional regulation. By observing emotions without immediately reacting, individuals develop a capacity to navigate emotional experiences with greater equanimity. This emotional resilience contributes to a more stable understanding of personal limits as reactions become more intentional and less impulsive.

The reflective nature of mindfulness practices prompts individuals to turn inward and explore their internal landscape. This improved self-reflection fosters a deeper understanding of personal values, needs, and priorities—all of which are integral components of establishing and communicating personal boundaries. And when these boundaries are recognized, individuals can learn to thrive within their limits, utilizing their strengths and overcoming their weaknesses.

At the same time, it is important to remember that mindfulness extends beyond individual awareness to interpersonal dynamics. By cultivating present-moment attention in social interactions, individuals develop a heightened sensitivity to others' cues and communication. This, in turn, contributes to more effective interpersonal boundary-setting and respect for the boundaries of others.

Exercises for Self-Reflection and Personal Development

Self-reflection and personal development are two essential aspects that lead you on the path to self-discovery. It is a path where introspection becomes the compass guiding you toward a more profound understanding of yourself and the world around you.

That said, here are some exercises that can help you indulge in the practices of self-reflection and personal development:

Journaling

Journaling stands as a timeless and invaluable tool for self-reflection, providing a sacred space to excavate the depths of our thoughts and emotions.

In the hustle of daily life, it serves as a deliberate pause, allowing you to unpack the intricacies of your experiences and chart the contours of your inner landscape.

The act of reflecting on gratitude fosters a positive mindset, encouraging you to acknowledge the blessings that often escape your hurried awareness. Conversely, pondering challenges becomes a compass for personal growth, offering insights into your resilience and problem-solving abilities.

Through the written word, you create a tangible record of your journey, a mirror reflecting your joys, struggles, and evolving narratives. Journaling is not merely a routine; it is a conscious commitment to self-discovery, illuminating the path toward a more intentional and mindful existence.

To integrate journaling into your daily or weekly routine, designate a specific time and space conducive to reflection. Start with simple prompts like "What am I grateful for today?" to redirect your focus toward positive aspects of your life.

Allow your thoughts to flow freely, unconstrained by judgment or perfectionism. Likewise, engage with prompts that inquire about challenges faced and solutions discovered, fostering a constructive mindset toward adversity.

Consider making journaling a ritual, perhaps over morning coffee or before bedtime, ensuring consistency.

Mindfulness Meditation

Mindfulness meditation serves as a profound gateway to present-moment awareness, a state where the mind is fully attuned to the unfolding now.

You can practice meditation by finding a quiet and comfortable space where you can sit or lie down without distractions. Close your eyes and bring your awareness to your breath. The practice of focusing on the breath anchors you to the current instant, a rhythmic reminder that each inhale and exhale exists only in the present.

As thoughts arise, observe them without attachment or judgment, letting them pass like clouds in the sky. Gently redirect your attention to the breath whenever the mind begins to wander, anchoring yourself in the present moment.

Start with short sessions, gradually extending the duration as you become more comfortable with the practice. Consider using guided mindfulness meditation apps or resources to provide structure and support, especially if you're new to the practice.

Consistency is key, so aim to incorporate mindfulness meditation into your daily routine, whether it's a few minutes in the morning or before bedtime. Over time, this intentional practice will foster a heightened sense of present-moment awareness, enhancing your overall well-being and mental clarity.

The Five Whys

The "Five Whys" technique, originating from lean manufacturing and later embraced in various problem-solving domains, holds immense value in unraveling the intricate layers of challenges you encounter.

At its core, this method encourages a relentless pursuit of the root cause by repeatedly asking "Why?" until the underlying issue is exposed.

When confronted with a challenge, initiate the "Five Whys" process by asking yourself, "Why is this happening?" Identify the apparent cause and then proceed to question why that circumstance exists.

Repeat this inquiry five times, systematically peeling away layers of causation.

For example, if the challenge is work-related, your first question might be, "Why did the project miss the deadline?" As you continue, you may uncover factors like insufficient resources, unclear instructions, or team communication issues. By the fifth "Why," you should arrive at the root cause, such as a lack of project management training.

Reflect on the insights gained and consider how addressing this fundamental issue can lead to more effective and enduring solutions.

This technique serves as a diagnostic tool for self-discovery, unveiling the complexities of your decision-making processes and guiding you toward a more comprehensive understanding of the factors influencing your actions.

Strengths Assessment

Understanding and leveraging our strengths is a cornerstone of personal development, contributing significantly to your overall well-being and fulfillment.

To do so, you can utilize tools such as the VIA Character Strengths Survey, a widely recognized tool in positive psychology. It offers a structured approach to identifying and categorizing individual strengths.

Recognizing and cultivating these strengths is crucial as it shifts the focus from fixing weaknesses to amplifying what inherently makes you thrive.

Begin by taking the VIA Character Strengths Survey to identify your top strengths. Reflect on the results, considering instances in your life when you have naturally demonstrated these strengths.

Pay attention to activities that energize you and make you feel engaged, as they often align with your strengths. Create a list of your key strengths and explore how you can intentionally apply them in different aspects of your life.

For example, if creativity is a strength, consider how you can infuse creativity into your work projects, hobbies, or problem-solving approaches. Regularly revisit and reassess your strengths, adapting them to new situations and challenges.

By consistently leveraging your strengths, you not only enhance your performance but also cultivate a sense of purpose and fulfillment, contributing to a more meaningful and satisfying life journey.

Gratitude Practice

The practice of regularly expressing gratitude is essential for cultivating a positive and resilient mindset.

While challenges and complexities dominate everyday life, the intentional act of acknowledging and appreciating what you are thankful for serves as a transformative shift in perspective.

Scientifically proven to enhance mental well-being, gratitude practice has been associated with reduced stress, increased feelings of happiness, and improved overall life satisfaction. By consciously directing your focus to the positive aspects of your life, even in the midst of difficulties, you train your mind to recognize and cherish the often-overlooked blessings that contribute to your daily experiences.

Incorporate this practice into your routine by setting aside a few minutes each day to reflect on and note three things you are thankful for. These can range from significant life events to small, everyday pleasures. Be specific in your expressions of gratitude, delving into the details of why each item holds significance for you.

Consider using a gratitude journal, where you record your thoughts and reflections consistently. If writing isn't your preferred mode of expression, incorporate gratitude into your daily routine by verbalizing your thanks aloud or silently reflecting during moments of quiet contemplation.

Experiment with different approaches to find what resonates with you. Over time, as this practice becomes a habit, you'll likely notice a positive shift in your mindset, fostering a heightened awareness of the richness and abundance present in your life.

Life Wheel Assessment

The life wheel is a powerful tool that provides a visual representation of various aspects of your life, offering a holistic perspective on your well-being. Each section of the wheel typically corresponds to key life domains such as career, relationships, health, and personal development.

So, start by creating or finding a life wheel template that resonates with you. Label each section with the key domains you want to assess, such as career, relationships, health, personal development, and more.

Reflect on each area and assign a score, considering how satisfied or fulfilled you currently feel in that domain. Use a numerical scale, like 1 to 10, to quantify your level of contentment.

Assessing the balance of these domains allows individuals to gain insight into the overall harmony of their lives. The importance lies in recognizing that personal growth extends beyond isolated achievements; it encompasses a harmonious integration of different facets.

Identify areas with lower scores or those that feel neglected. These are the domains that may need more attention for holistic personal growth. Set specific, realistic goals for improvement in those areas, and create an action plan outlining steps you can take to enhance your well-being in each domain.

Regularly revisit and reassess your life wheel, adjusting goals and strategies as needed. This ongoing practice enables you to maintain a dynamic and intentional approach to personal growth, ensuring that you cultivate a balanced and fulfilling life.

Silence and Solitude

Deliberately carving out moments of silence and solitude is a vital practice for nurturing inner peace and fostering self-discovery.

Amid the constant barrage of external stimuli, taking the intentional step to disconnect allows the mind to settle, creating a conducive space for introspection. This silence provides a canvas where your thoughts can unfold without external influence, offering a sanctuary for self-reflection and a deeper understanding of your own thoughts, emotions, and aspirations.

Choose a time and place where you won't be disturbed, free from the influence of electronic devices or external noise. Start with short sessions, perhaps 10 to 15 minutes, and gradually extend the duration as you become more comfortable with solitude.

Find a comfortable seated or lying position, close your eyes, and focus on your breath. Allow your thoughts to come and go without judgment, observing them like clouds passing through the sky.

If your mind wanders, gently redirect your focus to the present moment. Experiment with different forms of silent introspection, such as mindfulness meditation, contemplative walks, or simply sitting in nature.

Reflect on your experiences during these moments of solitude, considering any insights or revelations that arise. Making this practice a consistent part of your routine will cultivate a deeper connection with yourself, fostering self-discovery and contributing to a more centered and balanced life.

Incorporate the exercises and practices mentioned above into your routine based on your preferences and goals. Remember, consistency is key to reaping the benefits of self-reflection and fostering ongoing personal growth.

Chapter 12: Nurturing Respectful Boundaries in Life

A culture of respect for boundaries refers to an environment or society where individuals recognize and honor each other's personal, emotional, physical, and psychological limits. This culture is characterized by a mutual understanding that people have the right to set and maintain boundaries, and others should respect and not violate those boundaries.

More importantly, promoting a culture of respectful boundaries contributes to healthier relationships, increased well-being, and a more inclusive and empathetic society. It helps create an environment where everyone feels safe, valued, and free to express themselves authentically.

Let's understand the significance of this concept with the help of a story.

The Recovery of Respect: A Company's Transformation

In the bustling city of Los Angeles, California, there existed a company that aimed to reach sky-high. However, for years, the company was known for its toxic workplace culture. The air was thick with tension, and employees were pitted against each other in a cutthroat environment. The company's performance evaluation system promoted a hyper-competitive atmosphere, where colleagues were more likely to view each other as rivals rather than collaborators.

Furthermore, there was a prevailing expectation that employees should be available around the clock. Overtime was the norm, and burnout was widespread. If that wasn't enough, managers also exhibited a tendency to micromanage, stifling creativity and autonomy.

There were no clear boundaries regarding work expectations and personal time. The lack of defined limits contributed to an environment where employees felt constantly pressured to exceed their professional capacities, leading to heightened stress and dissatisfaction.

The toxic atmosphere had prevailed through several management changes, with each new leadership failing to address the underlying issues. However, a turning point arrived when a visionary leader, Cassie, assumed the role of the new CEO.

Cassie had a reputation for turning around struggling organizations, and her first order of business was to transform the company into a place where employees thrived rather than merely survived.

Upon her arrival, Cassie embarked on a comprehensive assessment of the workplace dynamics. She conducted anonymous surveys, held town hall meetings, and engaged in one-on-one conversations with employees. The feedback painted a stark picture of a toxic culture rooted in overworking, lack of communication, and a dearth of empathy.

With the data in hand, Cassie immediately implemented a series of changes. First and foremost, she revised the company's policies to prioritize work-life balance. Flexible working hours, remote work options, and clear expectations were introduced to foster a healthier environment. The new policies sent a clear message that the company valued the well-being of its employees.

To address communication breakdowns, Cassie initiated regular team-building exercises and training sessions focused on effective communication and conflict resolution. These activities aimed to break down the walls that had formed between departments and encourage collaboration.

One of the most significant changes involved leadership development programs. Managers underwent extensive training to enhance their emotional intelligence, empathy, and understanding of the importance of respecting boundaries. Cassie believed that change had to start at the top and cascade down through the entire organization.

As these changes took root, the transformation became tangible. Employees started expressing gratitude for the positive shifts in the workplace culture. A newfound sense of friendship emerged, and the toxic undercurrents that once prevailed began to dissipate.

Importance of Boundary Setting and Empathy in Organizations

Maintaining the delicate balance between individual boundaries and collective empathy is imperative for fostering positive environments.

Be it the workplace or community, research has consistently highlighted the importance of boundary-setting and empathy. From the bustling city offices to the heart of communities, the link between these two elements plays a pivotal role in shaping not only the well-being of individuals but also the overall success and harmony of the spaces they inhabit.

Let's look at some insightful research findings that showcase the importance of fostering respectful boundaries and empathy in organizations and communities.

Increased Productivity

The research conducted by Kossek et al. in 2015 delves into the intricate relationship between clear boundaries, productivity, and work-life balance in organizational settings. The findings underscore the transformative impact of well-defined boundaries on employee well-being and overall workplace effectiveness.

Clear boundaries provide employees with a structured framework for managing their time. When expectations regarding work hours, responsibilities, and communication channels are explicitly defined, individuals can allocate their time more efficiently.

Employees are better equipped to prioritize tasks, set realistic goals, and establish a work routine that aligns with organizational objectives. This enhanced time management contributes to increased productivity as individuals can focus on their core responsibilities without the ambiguity that often accompanies blurred boundaries.

Uncertainty about when to be available, what tasks take precedence, and how to balance work and personal life can create a heightened sense of anxiety. However, clear boundaries act as a stress-reducing mechanism by providing employees with a clear roadmap for their professional responsibilities.

Well-defined boundaries also contribute to a focused and concentrated work environment. Employees can immerse themselves in their tasks without the distraction of constantly shifting expectations or unclear guidelines.

The ability to concentrate on specific job responsibilities enhances task performance, quality of work, and overall efficiency. Employees can dedicate their attention to projects without the mental burden of navigating ambiguous boundaries.

The research also suggests that explicit boundaries facilitate better communication within teams. When individuals understand when and how to engage with their colleagues, collaboration becomes more streamlined and effective.

This improved communication promotes a positive team dynamic, fostering an environment where employees feel supported and connected. Team members can collaborate more effectively when expectations regarding availability and communication are clearly communicated.

Positive Work Environment

The research conducted by Dutton et al. in 2014 delves into the pivotal role of empathy in shaping positive work environments. The findings emphasize that organizations prioritizing empathy experience a myriad of positive outcomes, including heightened employee engagement, increased job satisfaction, and overall improved well-being.

Empathy fosters a sense of connection and understanding between colleagues and between employees and management. When individuals feel heard, valued, and understood, they are more likely to engage actively in their work.

Empathetic leaders and coworkers create an environment where employees feel a sense of belonging and shared purpose. This emotional connection contributes to increased enthusiasm, commitment, and involvement in organizational goals, ultimately leading to higher levels of employee engagement.

Furthermore, employees experiencing empathy from their colleagues and leadership are more likely to report higher job satisfaction. Feeling understood and supported in the workplace contributes to a positive attitude towards one's job, fostering a sense of fulfillment and contentment.

The study also indicates that the presence of empathy within an organization is linked to improved mental and emotional well-being among employees. When individuals perceive that their colleagues and leaders genuinely care about their concerns, stress levels decrease, and a positive mental health atmosphere is cultivated.

Empathy is instrumental in resolving conflicts in a constructive manner. When individuals understand and acknowledge each other's perspectives, conflicts are approached with a solution-oriented mindset rather than a confrontational one.

Organizations that prioritize empathy equip their teams with the skills to navigate disagreements, fostering a culture where conflicts are opportunities for growth and understanding rather than sources of tension and discord.

How to Foster Respectful Boundaries at Workplaces

In modern workplaces, where the lines between personal and professional life can sometimes blur, fostering an environment that respects and prioritizes boundaries is paramount. Recognizing the significance of maintaining a delicate balance between productivity and well-being, organizations are increasingly embracing strategies to create workplaces where individuals can thrive both professionally and personally.

This journey toward a culture of respectful boundaries requires a thoughtful and intentional approach, addressing not only the expectations within the workplace but also acknowledging the diverse needs and aspirations of the individuals who contribute to its success.

From leadership practices that set the tone for healthy boundaries to policies that prioritize work-life equilibrium, every aspect plays a crucial role in promoting a culture of respect.

That said, here are some tips that can help organizations foster respectful boundaries at work:

Clearly Define Expectations

Clear communication of job roles, responsibilities, and expectations is a foundational element in creating a work environment where employees can establish and maintain realistic boundaries for their workload and responsibilities.

Clearly articulate the specific responsibilities and tasks associated with each job role. This includes defining primary duties, reporting lines, and key performance indicators. When employees have a comprehensive understanding of what is expected of them, they can better manage their time and efforts.

Provide detailed job descriptions for each role within the organization. This document should outline the purpose of the role, essential duties, and qualifications required. Such clarity helps employees align their expectations with their actual responsibilities.

Clearly communicate performance expectations. Employees should be aware of the standards and benchmarks against which their performance will be evaluated. This transparency aids in setting realistic goals and boundaries as individuals strive to meet or exceed expectations.

When starting new projects, clearly outline timelines and deadlines. Employees can then manage their workload effectively, avoiding last-minute rushes and reducing the likelihood of work spilling into personal time.

Establish regular check-in sessions between employees and their supervisors. These meetings provide a forum for discussing current workloads, ongoing projects, and any challenges employees may be facing. Open communication enables early identification of potential issues and allows for timely adjustments to workload or expectations.

More importantly, when there are shifts in project priorities or changes in responsibilities, be sure to communicate these changes promptly and transparently. This allows employees to recalibrate their boundaries and make adjustments to their workload plans.

Promote Work-Life Balance

Encouraging a healthy work-life balance by setting reasonable working hours is a critical aspect of creating a workplace culture that values the well-being of its employees.

Clearly define standard working hours for employees. This clarity establishes a baseline for the expectations regarding when employees are expected to be actively engaged in work-related activities.

Strive for consistency across teams and departments when setting working hours. This helps in creating a unified organizational culture and ensures that all employees are aware of the standard expectations.

Communicate explicitly that constant availability after working hours is not an expectation. Set the tone from leadership down that employees are not obligated to respond to emails, calls, or work-related matters during their personal time.

Leadership should lead by example in respecting these boundaries. When leaders avoid sending non-urgent messages or scheduling meetings outside of standard working hours, it reinforces the organization's commitment to work-life balance.

But more than anything else, acknowledge and respect employees' personal time. Encourage them to fully disconnect during evenings, weekends, and holidays.

Constantly being on-call or expecting employees to be available around the clock can contribute to burnout. Recognize that employees need time to recharge, engage in personal activities, and spend quality time with family and friends.

Consider promoting the use of vacation days and paid time off. Establish a culture where employees feel encouraged to take the time off they are entitled to without feeling guilty or pressured to constantly be at their desks.

Flexible Working Arrangements

Implementing flexible working arrangements, such as remote work options or flexible hours, is a strategic initiative that empowers employees and contributes to a positive and adaptable workplace culture.

Remote work allows employees to integrate their professional responsibilities with their personal lives more seamlessly. It provides the flexibility to choose a work environment that suits individual preferences and enhances work-life balance.

Eliminating the need for daily commutes can significantly reduce stress and enhance well-being. Employees can use the time saved from commuting to engage in personal activities, contributing to a more fulfilling personal life.

Moreover, remote work opens the door to a broader talent pool by allowing organizations to hire individuals regardless of their geographical location. This can result in a more diverse and inclusive workforce.

On the other hand, flexible hours enable employees to align their work schedules with their natural productivity rhythms. Some individuals are more productive in the morning, while others may prefer working in the afternoon or evening. Allowing flexibility accommodates these preferences.

Employees can better balance personal and professional responsibilities when they have the freedom to adjust their working hours. This flexibility can lead to increased job satisfaction and reduced stress levels.

Besides, flexible hours can also accommodate personal commitments such as medical appointments, childcare responsibilities, or other obligations. This demonstrates organizational understanding and support for employees' diverse needs.

Consider utilizing cloud-based systems that allow employees to access work-related information and tools from anywhere. This ensures that individuals working remotely have the same level of access and functionality as those in the office.

But don't forget to establish clear communication channels to keep remote employees connected with their teams. Regular check-ins, virtual meetings, and transparent communication help maintain a sense of unity and purpose.

Training on Boundaries

Conducting training sessions on setting and respecting boundaries is a proactive and empowering approach to foster a culture of open communication and mutual respect in the workplace.

Design interactive workshops that educate employees on the importance of setting and respecting boundaries. Use real-life scenarios and case studies to illustrate how clear boundaries contribute to a healthier work environment.

Discuss the impact of boundaries on individual well-being, stress management, and overall job satisfaction. Help employees recognize that setting boundaries is not only acceptable but also crucial for maintaining a healthy work-life balance.

Provide training on effective communication techniques. Equip employees with the skills to express their needs, concerns, and boundaries in a clear and assertive manner, fostering an open and supportive dialogue.

You can also facilitate self-reflection activities to help employees identify their personal boundaries. Encourage them to consider their individual preferences, work styles, and limits, fostering self-awareness.

Guide employees in setting professional limits by defining their roles, expectations, and ideal working conditions. This includes discussing workload management, response times, and acceptable communication methods.

Allow teams to have discussions on establishing group norms regarding boundaries. Encourage teams to collaboratively define acceptable communication practices, meeting schedules, and expectations for responsiveness.

Integrate team-building activities that emphasize the importance of respecting each other's boundaries. These activities foster a sense of companionship and shared responsibility for maintaining a positive and supportive work environment.

Encourage Breaks

Breaks provide employees with an opportunity to step away from their work tasks, mentally refresh, and recharge. This brief pause helps prevent mental fatigue and maintains cognitive function and focus throughout the day.

Plus, breaks stimulate creativity and innovation. Stepping away from a problem or task can lead to fresh perspectives and new ideas when employees return to their work.

Leadership should endorse and model the importance of taking breaks. When leaders prioritize breaks, it sends a powerful message that well-being is valued within the organization.

Integrate break-friendly policies into the organizational culture. This includes explicit guidelines on break durations encouraging employees to utilize their allotted break times.

It's even better if you can provide flexibility in scheduling to accommodate breaks. Allow employees to plan their breaks at times that align with their natural energy rhythms and workload demands.

Consider establishing well-designed break areas that provide a comfortable and inviting environment. This could include comfortable seating, access to natural light, and recreational activities to encourage relaxation.

Besides, you can always encourage employees to use breaks as an opportunity to connect with colleagues, fostering a sense of camaraderie and team cohesion.

Promote Self-Care

Encouraging self-care practices is a proactive and compassionate approach that organizations can adopt to support the holistic well-being of their employees.

Start by establishing comprehensive wellness programs that encompass physical, mental, and emotional well-being. These programs can include fitness classes, nutrition workshops, mindfulness sessions, and stress reduction activities. Ensure that wellness programs are accessible to all employees, regardless of their role or work location. This may involve offering virtual sessions, providing on-site resources, or partnering with local wellness providers.

Provide access to Employee Assistance Programs that offer confidential counseling and mental health support services. EAPs can assist employees in addressing a range of personal and work-related challenges.

You can also offer subsidies for gym memberships or organize on-site fitness classes. Physical activity is a key component of overall well-being and can contribute to stress reduction and improved mental health.

More importantly, provide ergonomic workstations and encourage employees to take short breaks for stretching or brief walks. Physical comfort in the workplace positively impacts overall health.

Conduct regular check-ins with employees to discuss their well-being and work-related stressors. Individual check-ins provide an opportunity for personalized support and assistance.

Consider establishing anonymous feedback channels where employees can express their needs, concerns, or suggestions related to well-being. This allows for continuous improvement and responsiveness to evolving needs.

By integrating the strategies mentioned above, organizations can cultivate a workplace culture that values and respects boundaries, ultimately leading to higher employee satisfaction, improved well-being, and enhanced overall productivity.

Postface

Congratulations on reaching this far! As I conclude *Understanding Your Limits,* it is my sincerest hope that this book proved to be more than just a guidebook — I hope it has been a companion in your journey of self-discovery and growth.

Throughout the pages of this book, we embarked on a voyage through the diverse landscapes of human experience, delving into the world of personal and professional boundaries.

Keeping the lessons from this book in mind, be sure to celebrate the richness of your individuality and acknowledge your limits. Do not view limits as inadequacy; rather, think of them as the starting point for personal and professional elevation.

Life is a delicate balance between pushing your own boundaries and respecting the limits of others. As you navigate this landscape, be sure to foster collaboration, empathy, and ethical conduct.

This book is an invitation to live authentically, harmoniously, and within ethical bounds. Embrace your roles, competencies, and authorities with responsibility, contributing to the creation of a just, respectful, and harmonious society.

Recognize that your journey is one of continuous expansion. Each limit encountered is an opportunity for growth. Boldly push against these limits, not to erase them, but to reveal the vast capabilities that lie beyond.

As you close the final chapter, take moments to reflect on your own life, relationships, and professions. Apply the principles woven into these pages and evolve in your understanding of limits as a dynamic force that propels you toward a fulfilling existence.

Remember, your journey is boundless, and the wisdom gained from *Understanding Your Limits* is a guiding light. May your path be filled with self-discovery, resilience, and the joy of living authentically within your own boundaries.

Thank you for entrusting me with a part of your journey.

- Sami Dayriyeh

References

Baumeister, R. F., Vohs, K. D., & Tice, D. M. (2007). The Strength Model of Self-Control. Current Directions in Psychological Science, 16(6), 351-355. https://doi.org/10.1111/j.1467-8721.2007.00534.x

Bonanno, George A. "Loss, trauma, and human resilience: have we underestimated the human capacity to thrive after extremely aversive events?." *The American Psychologist* vol. 59,1 (2004): 20-8. doi: 10.1037/0003-066X.59.1.20

Hayes, Steven C et al. "Acceptance and commitment therapy: model, processes, and outcomes." Behaviour research and therapy vol. 44,1 (2006): 1-25. doi: 10.1016/j.brat.2005.06.006

Langenberg, D.N. (2000). Teaching children to read: An evidence-based assessment of the scientific research literature on reading and its implications for reading instruction.

Heimberg RG, Mueller GP, Holt CS, Hope DA, Liebowitz MR. Assessment of anxiety in social interaction and being observed by others: the Social Interaction Anxiety Scale and the Social Phobia Scale. Behavior Therapy. 1992;23(1):53–73. https://doi.org/10.1016/S0005-7894(05)80308-9

Cain, S. (2012). "Quiet: The power of introverts in a world that can't stop talking." Crown.

Seligman, Martin & Csikszentmihalyi, Mihaly. (2000). Positive Psychology: An Introduction. The American psychologist. 55. 5-14. 10.1037/0003-066X.55.1.5.

Kabeer, N. (2005). Gender equality and women's empowerment: A critical analysis of the third-millennium development goal 1. Gender & Development, 13(1), 13–24. https://doi.org/10.1080/13552070512331332273

Duflo, Esther. 2012. "Women Empowerment and Economic Development." Journal of Economic Literature, 50 (4): 1051-79. http://www.jstor.org/stable/23644911

Gollwitzer, Peter & Oettingen, Gabriele. (2011). Planning Promotes Goal Striving. Handbook of Self-Regulation: Research, Theory, and Applications.

Gabbard, G. O. (1994). Psychodynamic Psychiatry in Clinical Practice: The DSM-IV Edition. American Psychiatric Pub.

American Psychological Association. (2017). Ethical Principles of Psychologists and Code of Conduct. https://www.apa.org/ethics/code

Corey, G., Corey, M. S., & Callanan, P. (2018). Issues and Ethics in the Helping Professions. Cengage Learning.

Twenge, Jean M, and W Keith Campbell. "Associations between screen time and lower psychological well-being among children and adolescents: Evidence from a population-based study." Preventive Medicine Reports vol. 12 271-283. 18 Oct. 2018, doi: 10.1016/j.pmedr.2018.10.003

Buchanan, Tom & Joinson, Adam & Paine Schofield, Carina & Reips, Ulf-Dietrich. (2007). Development of measures of online privacy concern and protection for use on the Internet. Journal of the American Society for Information Science and Technology. 58. 157-165. https://doi.org/10.1002/asi.20459

Firth, Joseph, et al. "The efficacy of smartphone-based mental health interventions for depressive symptoms: a meta-analysis of randomized controlled trials." World Psychiatry: Official Journal of the World Psychiatric Association (WPA) vol. 16,3 (2017): 287-298. https://doi.org/10.1002/wps.20472

Blendon, Robert J et al. "Views of practicing physicians and the public on medical errors." The New England Journal of Medicine vol. 347,24 (2002): 1933-40. doi: 10.1056/NEJMsa022151

Brennan, T A et al. "Incidence of adverse events and negligence in hospitalized patients. Results of the Harvard Medical Practice Study I." The New England Journal of Medicine vol. 324,6 (1991): 370-6. doi: 10.1056/NEJM199102073240604

Merry, Sally & Silbey, Susan. (1984). What Do Plaintiffs Want? Reexamining the Concept of Dispute. Justice System Journal. 9. 151-178.

"Gray, Cheryl W.; Kaufman, Daniel. 1998. Corruption and Development. PREM Notes; No. 4. © World Bank, Washington, DC. http://hdl.handle.net/10986/11545

"Trust and Distrust in America." 2019. Pew Research Center

Besley, Timothy & Prat, Andrea. (2006). Handcuffs for the Grabbing Hand? Media Capture and Government Accountability. American Economic Review. 96. 720-736.

Leonardo Tavares. Healing the Codependency (2023).

Parks, M.R. and Floyd, K. (1996) Making Friends in Cyberspace. Journal of Communication, 46, 80-97.
https://doi.org/10.1111/j.1460-2466.1996.tb01462.x

Aurélien, G., & Melody, M. (2019). A Theory of Guilt Appeals: A Review Showing the Importance of Investigating Cognitive Processes as Mediators between Emotion and Behavior. Behavioral sciences (Basel, Switzerland), 9(12), 117.
https://doi.org/10.3390/bs9120117

Mayer, R. C., Davis, J. H., & Schoorman, F. D. (1995). An Integrative Model of Organizational Trust. The Academy of

Management Review, 20(3), 709–734.
https://doi.org/10.2307/258792

Olthof, T. & Smeets-Schouten, Anneke & Kuiper, Hilde & Stegge, Hedy & Jennekens-Schinkel, Aag. (2000). Shame and Guilt in children: Differential situational antecedents and experiential correlates. British Journal of Developmental Psychology. 18. 51 - 64. https://doi.org/10.1348/026151000165562

Carroll, Archie. (1999). Corporate social responsibility: Evolution of a definitional construct. Business & Society. 38. 268-295.

Kossek, Ellen & Ruderman, Marian & Braddy, Phillip & Hannum, Kelly. (2012). Work–nonwork boundary management profiles: A person-centered approach. Journal of Vocational Behavior. 81. 112–128. https://doi.org/10.1016/j.jvb.2012.04.003

Björk-Fant, J. M., Bolander, P., & Forsman, A. K. (2023). Work-life balance and work engagement across the European workforce: a comparative analysis of welfare states. European journal of public health, 33(3), 430–434.
https://doi.org/10.1093/eurpub/ckad046

Kreiner, G. E., Hollensbe, E. C., & Sheep, M. L. (2009). Balancing Borders and Bridges: Negotiating the Work-Home Interface via Boundary Work Tactics. Academy of Management Journal, 52(4), 704–730. https://doi.org/10.5465/amj.2009.43669916

Sheldon, K. M., & Kasser, T. (2001). Goals, Congruence, and Positive Well-Being: New Empirical Support for Humanistic Theories. Journal of Humanistic Psychology, 41(1), 30-50.
https://doi.org/10.1177/0022167801411004

Grant, Anthony & Franklin, John & Langford, Peter. (2002). The Self-Reflection and Insight Scale: A New Measure of Private Self-Consciousness. Social Behavior and Personality: an international

journal. 30. 821-835.
https://doi.org/10.2224/sbp.2002.30.8.821

Kabat-Zinn, J. (1990). Full catastrophe living: Using the wisdom of your body and mind to face stress, pain, and illness. New York, NY: Delacorte.

Kossek, Ellen Ernst, and Rebecca J. Thompson, 'Workplace Flexibility: Integrating Employer and Employee Perspectives to Close the Research–Practice Implementation Gap', in Tammy D. Allen, and Lillian T. Eby (eds), *The Oxford Handbook of Work and Family*, Oxford Library of Psychology (2016; online edn, Oxford Academic, 3 Feb. 2015), https://doi.org/10.1093/oxfordhb/9780199337538.013.19

Dutton, Jane & Workman, Kristina & Hardin, Ashley. (2014). Compassion at Work. Annual Review of Organizational Psychology and Organizational Behavior. 1. 277-304. 10.1146/annurev-orgpsych https://doi.org/10.1146/annurev-orgpsych-031413-091221

About the Author

Sami Dayriyeh is a seasoned professional with a remarkable career spanning over four decades in engineering and management. With an undergraduate degree in engineering and master's degrees in management, law, and arbitration, he possesses a unique blend of technical expertise and strategic vision.

Throughout his professional journey, Sami has had the opportunity to work in numerous countries, immersing himself in diverse cultures and gaining a profound understanding of global business dynamics. His international experience has not only shaped his professional growth but also helped him learn more about leadership, innovation, bias in human interactions, the importance of boundaries, and problem-solving.

Throughout his career, Sami has prioritized continuous learning and personal growth, always seeking opportunities to expand his limits and embrace new challenges. His passion for understanding different cultures and business practices has fueled his drive to excel in his field and become a leader.

As an author, Sami brings his wealth of experience and diverse background to the table. He is dedicated to sharing his insights and lessons learned.

Through his writing, he aims to inspire individuals to embrace continuous learning, understand problems, mitigate bias, and thrive within their limits without feeling pressured into crossing the line.

Currently, Sami has written *Shaping Your Success, Simplifying Complexities, Subconsciously Biased, Unbound Learning, Engage Your Mind, Enrich Your Life,* and *Understanding Your Limits.* Through these literary gems, he illuminates diverse facets of life.

Printed in Great Britain
by Amazon

bfa0381b-fb02-41ff-8986-32bddcdd0f6aR01